Ettore Sottsass Jnr

PENNY SPARKE
The Design Council

Ettore Sottsass Jnr

First edition published in the United Kingdom
1982 by The Design Council, 28 Haymarket
London SW1Y 4SU

Printed and bound in the United Kingdom by
The Whitefriars Press Limited

British Library CIP Data

Sparke, Penny
    Ettore Sottsass Jnr.
    1. Sottsass, Ettore
    I. Title
    745.2   TS79

    ISBN 0-85072-126-1

Contents

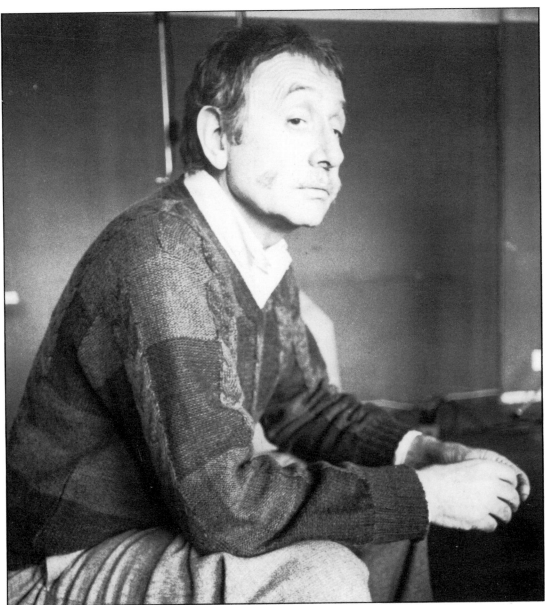

STEPHEN BAYLEY

Ettore Sottsass Jnr as he is today, still living and working in the heart of Milan.

Preface

It is, of course, very pleasing to have a book as beautiful as Penny's written all about oneself. We are always egocentric enough to be delighted by such an event and to believe that, if there is such a book, there must be some truth in it. But because we always want to find truth in our lives, there is also the fear that there may not be any, or hardly any – or perhaps that what seems true to us will, to an outsider and in the final analysis, amount to nothing. Still, the fact that Penny has written this book so well, that somebody thought it was possible to produce it so beautifully, and that the whole project has materialised is most consoling and encouraging for me, and I would like to thank everybody for it.

The other side of the coin is that a book such as this is also very dangerous. A book is not real life: the daily grind, the anxiety, the confusion, the excuses of a headache or the radio that would not let you work in peace, the thousands of cards covered with sketches that seemed so brilliant because you never risked finishing them, and all those other distractions for which there are always friendly opiates (the doctors' endomorphines) to make you feel better . . . in a finished book these things are no longer apparent.

A book is definite. Everything is reduced to its essentials. There are no dark corners in which to hide (alas!), and for that reason its subject feels a little dead – perhaps, who knows, as one may when the spirit slips slowly away. With a book one feels stripped bare of one's coat, trousers, shirt and pants, standing naked in front of everybody. One feels a bit like a newly shorn sheep or a bedraggled fledgling. And this is my second reaction to having a book written about me.

And then there is yet another, a third reaction. This is a feeling of freedom from oneself, as if you have packed all your possessions in a suitcase – passport, childhood photographs and all – put the case in the middle of the room, closed the windows and door and walked out of the house, leaving it all for someone else. From that moment you turn to new horizons, you travel and explore, looking for new challenges because you have been freed from the past. This nomadic way of coping with internal and external events is the one that I myself prefer. I always like to strive, as children do, right up to the limits that my circumstances impose. Perhaps I am apologising for it, but that is the way I am. Maybe that is why I never stay long in one place, and why I have never had really fixed ideas. I can only stay sitting at my drawing board for a few hours and then I have to move. Perhaps for this reason I have never tried to confront deep issues such as the future of man, nations and cities, or great architecture or historic monuments and things of that kind. This is why I have always made small things, things in which we take a passing interest, things we handle for a moment and then put down – amulets, perhaps, to wear on our travels, which may not even be worth leaving behind for posterity.

In any case, for this third sort of feeling that comes from having a book written about me, I must again thank Penny and all those who have helped with the book's production. I must thank them because they have provided me with the best possible way of taking me out of myself – of making me change my path and set off again in another direction . . . if all this is really possible.

Ettore Sottsass Jnr
March 1982

Introduction

'It would be difficult to make a catalogue of my work because I have never made monuments for the public drama, only fragile sets for private theatre, for private meditation and solitude.'

E. Sottsass Jnr

Ettore Sottsass Jnr lives and works in Milan, the city that supports the highest concentration of important living designers in Italy and probably in the world. Aged 64, he is one of the most fascinating designers living today. Since the mid-1960s his progressive and uncompromising attitude has inspired several generations of students of design and practising designers who sought, and still seek, new solutions to new problems.

The presence of Sottsass is felt in many of the more interesting objects that make up the contemporary environment. It was he, for example, who put colour into mechanical and electronic equipment and humour into furniture and it is thanks to him, more than to any other single designer, that the 'black box' is currently being replaced by forms and symbols that take into account the human beings who use them as well as the technology that engendered them.

Sottsass' reputation has come through to the English-speaking world in fits and starts, and for this reason he is surrounded by a layer of popular mythology and confusion. He is, for some, an eccentric mystic preoccupied with introducing strange, esoteric philosophies into the language of design; for others, the creative impulse behind so many of the sophisticated, sensuous office machines produced by the Olivetti company; and, for still others, the man behind Italian radical design. In reality he is all of these and more besides, and this study of his life and career illustrates the unity of purpose behind these varied myths.

I came across the designs of Ettore Sottsass at first hand rather late in the day, at an exhibition of his work in Paris in 1976. The radicalism and variety of his designs – which ranged from jewellery to ceramics to industrial design to furniture to glass – were astonishing, as was the feeling of unity behind this plurality. Having decided that the lesson from this body of work, which combined instinctive sensuousness with rigorous intellectualism, was one that needed to be communicated to an English-speaking audience, I began to investigate it further and realised, when I met Sottsass two years later (the first of many meetings), that his contribution to contemporary culture could not be reduced to that of a designer alone but that he is also a philosopher, a poet, an art critic and a fine artist: someone who responds to, appreciates, understands and communicates the fine things of life.

In true Italian Renaissance style, Sottsass moves across a broad cultural spectrum and this small book cannot encompass all that that implies. Instead it concentrates upon Ettore Sottsass – theorist and practitioner of design, while at the same time placing him within the broader context of Italian design of the post-Second World War years. In doing this I hope to emphasise both his radicalism and his essential 'Italianness'. It would have been hard, if not impossible, for such a designer to have emerged from any other country in these years.

Post-war Italian design is, as we all know from the glossy magazines that showed it to us in the 1950s, 1960s and 1970s, represented by luxurious, sculptural, high-gloss, highly-finished domestic objects that smack of the 'good life' and exploit new materials, particularly plastics. Although Sottsass lived and worked in Milan, the centre of this design explosion through these three decades, he stands apart from this image of Italian design: he is at once more complex and more abstract. Sottsass' philosophy of modern life and culture is expressed not only through his designs but also in a vast output of critical and creative writings.

The nature of Sottsass' personality is at the root of his being largely unknown and misrepresented. Unlike many of his 'superstar' contemporaries Sottsass refuses work if it doesn't conform to his personal convictions, and thus much of his output is in limited production only, maybe only at the prototype stage. He works, like a fine artist, to develop his creative consciousness and this unfailing integrity has earned him the respect of many young people who have, over the years, travelled to Milan, nursing high hopes of being able to work beside him in his studio.

Sottsass has been practising as a designer for over 30 years and has had a front-seat view of many important design changes in that period. His career falls neatly into three phases between 1945 and the present, and the structure of this book reflects those stages in his life.

Sottsass says he became a designer because:

I didn't want to teach in a school because I thought that I did not have anything to teach, as I considered myself a man who still had everything to try; I couldn't find a job by myself, for myself, because to be an architect, a free professional man, is a luxury job, it is an intellectual job that the middle class pays only against guarantees, the slightest of which is to show – at least – a little money already owned and invested in the setting up of a professional office, with telephone, secretary, draughtsmen etc; plus a car, while I owned only a bicycle ... I thought at that time that it was really possible to be a craftsman.[1]

A striking idealism characterises Sottsass' attitude in this early period, as it did those of his contemporaries. Designing interiors for friends and writing about art and design pointed the way forward, and he grasped the challenge with both hands, following his heart at all times rather than his head.

Sottsass' entire creative career is characterised by an intuitive rejection of the anonymous 'functional' style of the pre-Second World War years. The European architecture of the inter-war years, particularly in Germany and France, had been dominated by a style epitomised by abstract geometric form, simplicity, anonymity, lack of decoration and features such as white walls, ribbon windows and flat roofs. Deriving from forms originated by the Cubist painters, this school of architecture became known as Functionalism (the Italian version of the same style was referred to as Rationalism).

Sottsass sought first for an alternative aesthetic and later for an alternative theory of design (whether for furniture, jewellery, architecture, ceramics, graphics, paintings or industrial products) that puts man at the centre. Sottsass was and is essentially a sign-maker, creating an environment in which custom, ritual, use and love define man's interaction with objects and help to determine his life-style. From the early days Sottsass saw the creation of form, not in terms of a superficial or stylistic exercise, but as a fundamental means of manipulating raw materials in a 'sensorial' way, providing a symbolic link between man and object. (Sottsass uses the word 'sensorial' frequently to denote his intention of appealing directly to people's senses through his objects.)

During the early 1950s Sottsass was temporarily seduced by the sensuous shapes of contemporary industrially produced objects and moved, along with his contemporaries, towards an emotive, sculptural style as a ploy against perpetuating the Rationalist aesthetic. He was quick to see, however, the cul-de-sac of status that this evasive tactic implied and moved, after his trips to the USA in 1956 and to India in 1961, towards a less formal and more spiritual involvement with functional objects. It is Alessandro Mendini who has best described Sottsass' work of this period: 'He works with primary signs, child-like markings: the circle, the cylinder; he needs only lines and dots to obtain any level of sophistication ... no stylistic form, no functional approach.'[2]

In this second phase of his career, Sottsass' philosophy of objects stands out in sharp contrast to the mainstream of Italian design from this period. Elitist, highly styled and status ridden, the work of most of his contemporaries betrayed values with which Sottsass refused to be associated. His fundamentally humanistic outlook encouraged him to move further towards 'meaning' and away from 'style' in the objects he designed: towards a conception of design that reflected the world of man and of nature, perceived and translated through sensory rather than rational filters. (Reyner Banham commented in an article in the *New Statesman* in the early 1960s that Sottsass chose to drive a Ford Anglia rather than a highly styled Italian car, as a deliberate antidote to prevailing Italian chic.)

In his individualistic rejection of the dominant forces in Italian design of the late 1950s and early 1960s, Sottsass anticipated the radicalism of the late 1960s. He is hailed by many as the father of Counter-Design or Anti-Design – convenient labels for a movement which Sottsass would not categorise so formally.

In working through the development of Sottsass' *oeuvre* what will emerge most strongly will be the evolution of a personal language. He uses objects to communicate his creative consciousness to the world and the story of his designs mirrors the changes in his own mental and emotional reactions to life. Although he likes to think of himself as an 'intellectual nomad' and denies any consistency in his career, I hope that the following pages will refute this belief and suggest instead that the genius of Ettore Sottsass lies in the continuity and consistency of his commitment to design.

Reconstruction and Design

In Italy the decade after the Second World War was characterised by the rapid and enthusiastic recreation of a culture that had been eclipsed by Fascism and which by 1945 showed few signs of having survived the holocaust of war. The role of design in this period was crucial: it symbolised the character of Italian aspirations, manifest in rapid industrial expansion and in the search for a new aesthetic for the everyday environment.

A vivid picture of the poverty in Italy at the end of the war – evident in both the social and the design contexts – is presented in the pages of *Domus,* a magazine dedicated to architecture and design. During the years 1946 and 1947 its editor, the architect Ernesto N. Rogers, preached the double-headed doctrine of architectural Rationalism and anti-Fascism. Italy had been physically devastated by the war and the task in hand, as perceived by Rogers and many of his contemporaries, was a programme of rapid reconstruction on the industrial, economic, cultural and architectural fronts simultaneously. Rogers saw the immediate role of *Domus* as that of playing a strong ideological part in his country's reconstruction. With this in mind, he wrote in the January 1946 edition: 'It is a question of forming a taste, a technique, a morality, all terms of the same function. It is a question of building a society.'[3]

The birth pangs of this new aesthetic, which was to combine pre-war Rationalism with organic form, were felt for several years and *Domus* demonstrates the split in interests of this period by including in its pages, as early as 1947, images of the Surrealistic fantasies of the Turin furniture-maker Carlo Mollino alongside more functionally oriented discussions about standardisation, prefabrication and the economics of the production of useful furniture for small living spaces. Rogers himself came down on the side of the Rationalist aesthetic,

although he redefined it by integrating architecture and design further into the general context of culture as a whole.

Gio Ponti, on the other hand, who succeeded Rogers as editor in 1948, took a softer line over the alliance between architectural and social theory, preferring to see design as an aesthetic phenomenon first and foremost and its role in society as one of providing increased comfort and the possibilities of an easy and affluent lifestyle. His essentially bourgeois stance was to have a strong influence on Italian attitudes towards design in the following 20 years.

OFFICE OF RAY AND CHARLES EAMES

Charles Eames's chair was designed, with the help of Eero Saarinen, in 1946. Its aesthetic and technical innovations inspired many of the young architect-designers in Milan when it appeared in Domus *in the late 1940s.*

The work of the young architects in Turin and Milan – Marco Zanuso, Vico Magistretti, Roberto Menghi, Alberto Rosselli, the Castiglioni brothers and many others who had trained in the architectural schools in the 1930s under the dominance of Rationalism – soon became an intrinsic part of the cultural regeneration in these years. They responded to the visual stimuli from abroad illustrated in *Domus* and to the new economic and social conditions. Funds were too scarce for extensive architectural projects, so these young men turned their attentions to the obvious next choice, architectural accessories, furniture and other pieces of domestic equipment. They were particularly responsive to the possibilities opened to them in the new consumer product industries that had been expanding rapidly since the war; such products provided a challenge for this generation whose talents were, as yet, untested. They all tried their hand at mass production working with new materials – plywood, aluminium, glass and later plastics – producing designs that displayed a self-consciousness of form as yet unwitnessed in Italian consumer goods.

The main bulk of production lay within the furniture area, where experiments (influenced by the Americans Charles Eames and Eero Saarinen) of joining metal to wood became commonplace, and the organic curves derived from contemporary sculpture became a familiar sight in the Milanese living room by the end of the 1940s.

Examples of 'industrial design' from this period are few, but highly significant, since they point towards a style – as yet only emerging – which by the early 1960s came to epitomise Italian design for the rest of the world. Gio Ponti's coffee machine designed for La Pavoni and produced in 1948 owes much to the bulbous styling of commercial objects from the other

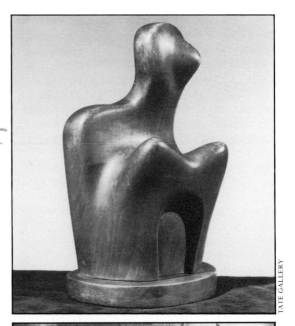

TATE GALLERY

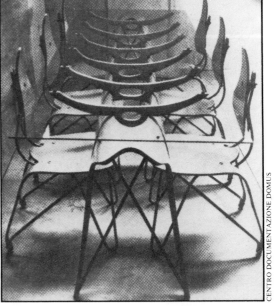

CENTRO DOCUMENTAZIONE DOMUS

Opposite, top: This figure of 1931 by Henry Moore is characteristic of the organic forms that appeared in Domus *in the late 1940s and which had a strong effect on the young architects, bored with the geometry of Rationalism.*
Opposite, bottom: Carlo Mollino's fantastic designs for furniture are reminiscent of organic shapes. Produced in Turin through the 1940s and 1950s, they represent an extreme example of the prevailing interest in expressive form.
Below: By the beginning of the 1950s the architect and editor of Domus, *Gio Ponti, had produced a vast range of designs including furniture, a car and a number of smaller objects. This cutlery was manufactured by Krupp and exhibited at the Ninth Triennale in 1951.*
Right: Trained as an architect in the 1930s, Marco Zanuso turned, after the war, to furniture and industrial design. This chair, from the late 1940s, reflects a concern with cheap, practical furniture for the post-war home.

CENTRO DOCUMENTAZIONE DOMUS

GIO PONTI

side of the Atlantic, but also has a visual restraint and elegance uncharacteristic of American products. Italian designs for transport, such as the Vespa motor scooter designed by Piaggio in 1946 and the Lambretta designed in the following year, and car designs by PininFarina, were similarly elegant in their aesthetic solutions. They all serve to demonstrate how body styling need not be brash, nor solely commercial in its intention. Marcello Nizzoli's work for the Olivetti company – for example the Lexikon 80 typewriter of 1948 – reinforces this commitment to simple, sculptured body shells concealing highly sophisticated, mechanical objects.

The support system for design also expanded considerably in these years, ranging from sponsorship by established companies such as the fabric firm of Fede Cheti to the assistance given by new firms such as Arflex, Azucena and Kartell; the reintroduction of the Milan

GIO PONTI

Triennales from 1947 onwards provided a major platform from which Italian 'flair' could display itself to the rest of the world.

The Eighth Triennale of 1947 had a strong social emphasis, focusing on the problem of the post-war home. A critic wrote in *Domus* that year, 'The programme of the Eighth Triennale had to take into account the social and economic climate created by the war ... It must face and solve problems which interest the least well-off classes.'[4]

By 1951 this conviction was already less in evidence and the theme of the Ninth Triennale – 'The Form of the Useful' – had an obviously aesthetic bias, proudly displaying the beautiful industrial products from the late 1940s. In 1954 the following Triennale put an even more deliberate emphasis upon the visual rather than the social impact of design, as demonstrated by its title, 'The Production of Art'. The exhibition showed 'abandoned playfulness' to be the aesthetic of the day: the products displayed were characterised by an unrestrained aesthetic and technical experimentation. Plastics, foam rubber, glass, wood and metal were all in evidence, manipulated with a greater formal freedom than ever before. Influences from fine art – particularly Organic Surrealism – were by now firmly integrated into the appearance of many of the objects and their settings, signalling

CENTRO DOCUMENTAZIONE DOMUS

PHOTO BALLO & BALLO

CARROZZERIA PININFARINA, TORINO

Opposite: Ponti's coffee machine for La Pavoni of 1949 was mentioned in Design *magazine by H.J.K. Henrion, who had noticed a family likeness among a number of Italian industrial products.*

Above left: Piaggio's design for the Vespa motor scooter of 1946 is another example of the new Italian industrial design aesthetic. It had more in common with products such as hairdriers and typewriters than with objects of transportation.

Below left: A designer who put post-war Italian automobile design on the map was PininFarina, whose sensuous, sculptured forms provided a visual alternative to the chrome excesses found in the USA. He designed the Cisitalia in 1946.

Above: The Lexikon 80, designed by Marcello Nizzoli for Olivetti in 1948, was one of the first typewriters with a sculptured shell. Nizzoli was Olivetti's consultant designer through the 1940s and 1950s, responsible for many notable designs, among them the Lettera 22 typewriter of 1950.

the final death blow to the Rationalist tendencies of the pre-war and early post-war years.

The American industrial designer, Walter Dorwin Teague, who visited Italy in 1950 to select some objects for an exhibition, described the general trend in Italian design in the years following the war: 'Since the war the artists have been frolicking like boys let out of school.'[5]

It was within this atmosphere of enthusiasm and fertile imagination that Ettore Sottsass Jnr began his career as a designer.

New Designs for a New Society

'Function is only one facet of the materials which men use and perceive.'
Gaetano Pesce

Ettore Sottsass Jnr began his career as an architect/designer in the aftermath of the Second World War, determined to challenge the double heritage of Rationalism and Fascism. The decade after 1945 was, for him, a formative period in which he allied himself with the prevailing taste for borrowing forms and patterns from the contemporary fine arts – notably Surrealism and organic sculpture – and was generally absorbed into the regenerative atmosphere of the time. He spent much of his time during this early period working on interiors for rich clients in Milan, but also found time for more personal researches into the formal qualities of the environment which in turn were transformed into objects for mass manufacture.

The period was characterised by relentless trial and error, an enthusiasm that comes with the energy of youth, and a level of confidence and sophistication surprising in someone setting out on a new career. Most of all, the designs from this period show an open-mindedness that enabled Sottsass to go on to expand his personal definition of design and to question the conventions and assumptions in which it was rooted.

When, like many of his contemporaries, Sottsass turned from a training in architecture to an involvement with designed objects, this change of direction was caused, not simply by the economic pressures of post-war Italy, but by a deep-seated desire to overturn the values of his parents' generation which he saw epitomised in the Italian architectural profession.

Ettore Sot-Sas Snr, an Austrian by birth, had trained under Otto Wagner in Vienna and become a successful architect in the Rationalist tradition. He moved from Trento to Turin with his family in 1928 and became a major protagonist in the architectural debate between Piacentini and Pagano over the project for Florence Station in the 1930s. Success as an architect implied many things to his son, both culturally and professionally. It meant acceptance of a middle-class set of values as well as adherence to the current visual idiom, both of which he saw as restrictions on personal liberty.

Sottsass Jnr's earliest creative outlet took the form of sketching, painting and sculpture and these initiated a lifelong enquiry into the nature of two- and three-dimensional plastic form – the quest of the fine artist rather than of the jobbing architect. He followed in his father's footsteps to the extent of attending the School of Architecture in the Polytechnic of Turin between 1934 and 1939, but he devoted many of his formative years to general creative activities that were to lead him in several different directions.

While he was a student colour was central to Sottsass' ideas about form, whether in two or three dimensions; and his theories concerning colour as a creator of space and its application to interior decoration appeared in the periodical *Lambello* in the late 1930s. Colour signified a liberation from the monochrome, structure-ridden space of the Rationalists and provided a direct link between painting and architecture. In 1936 Sottsass saw work by Picasso and Matisse in Paris, and in the next year met, in Turin, a painter called Spazzapan who was to become his mentor in matters concerning the spatial qualities of colour. The major influences upon Sottsass at this time were undoubtedly avant-garde painters: he was open to a broad spectrum of approaches from the Neo-Plasticists – those painters, architects and designers (among them Mondrian, van Doesburg and Oud) who formed the De Stijl group in Holland after the First World War and who had evolved an abstract aesthetic based on compositions made up of horizontal and vertical lines and the colours red, blue, yellow, black and white – to the more emotive concerns of painters such as Kandinsky. Spazzapan also introduced Sottsass to the work of Dufy and to the notion of Gesture painting which provided the young artist with another means of two-dimensional form-making – this time guided by the hand rather than by the mind. Sottsass' involvement with these painters was of an intuitive rather than an intellectual nature; he seized upon all of them as possible escape routes from the rigid laws of Rationalism.

After graduating from the Polytechnic of Turin, Sottsass worked for a short time at the Fiat carriage-works in the same city. The war then brutally interrupted his career, as it did those of so many architect-designers of his generation, and he spent the years from 1939 to 1945 in the services. Few possibilities for creativity presented themselves during this time, but Sottsass persisted. He began by painting portraits and later, in 1943, when he was based in Montenegro with the Alpine troops, produced some designs for cloth that were printed by local craftsmen. These years also served to encourage his interest in rustic, folk traditions which began during his childhood in the mountains. In 1945 he joined the Giuseppe Pagano group of architects in Turin and produced his first project for a home, continuing at the same time to pursue his interests in sculpture and in two-dimensional design in the form of designs for book covers and scarves. At the end of the year he left Turin and went to Milan which was rapidly becoming an artistic centre; there he began the first phase of his career as a practising architect-designer.

The prevailing atmosphere of regeneration in Milan, created on one side by *Domus* and on the other hand by the rapid expansion of industry, enthused Sottsass and he eagerly entered the frequent debates about the new aesthetic and a new role for architecture and the industrially produced object. His continuing search for a language of form manifested itself in his paintings, sculptures and in his prolific writings. With Bruno Munari he organised the first international show of abstract art in Milan, and in the exhibition catalogue outlined his theories of form, emphasising the abstract gesture in painting and the manipulation of space in sculpture.

The influence of the sculptor Max Bill, a friend at this time, was crucial in the development of Sottsass' ideas about space. His work moved towards a synthesis of ideas about abstraction derived from Neo-Plasticism combined with the more spontaneous and dynamic shapes characteristic of the Surrealists – Max Ernst, Jean Arp, Alexander Calder and Naum Gabo. In attempting to unite these approaches Sottsass stood at the centre of the Italian design consciousness at this period.

Pieces of sculpture produced in this period include a construction in wood, no 12145 of 1945, which consists of a Neo-Plastic, wooden grid juxtaposed with squares and cylinders. The same aesthetic formula is applied to an interior designed for a young girl in 1946 in which the rectilinear emphasis of the wood and metal shelving system resembles the construction of the previous year. In constructions no 08845 and 091647, both made of metal, dynamic curves and diagonals replace the grid of the previous year and dominate these abstract three-dimensional forms. These in turn are echoed in furniture for the Milan Triennale of 1947 and the Grassotti publicity stand for a Turin exhibition in 1948. In designs such as these, Sottsass' work stands alongside that of Carlo Mollino in its emphasis on expressive and organic form. Organic curves in laminated plywood create a sensuous mood in these designs and set the tone for the aesthetic idiom that will dominate the work of the next decade.

SOTTSASS ASSOCIATI

Right: Sottsass worked for a brief period for the Fiat carriage-works. These designs for handles of 1944 show his concern with organic sculptural form.
Below: While serving in the Italian army during the Second World War, Sottsass spent some time with the Alpine troops in Montenegro. The simple, rustic, peasant dwellings that he saw there had a strong impact on him, and determined many of his ideas about domestic architecture in the 1950s.

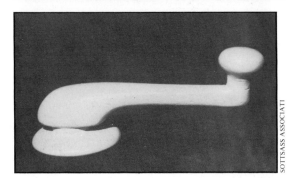

SOTTSASS ASSOCIATI

SOTTSASS ASSOCIATI

MAX BILL

SOTTSASS ASSOCIATI

TATE GALLERY

Above left: Among the European sculptors who had a strong influence on Sottsass in the post-war period was Max Bill, who created abstract, organic forms from industrial materials. This piece is from 1948.

Below left: This piece by Naum Gabo, entitled 'Linear Construction', represents the kind of Constructivist sculpture that Sottsass would have seen illustrated in periodicals in Italy of the 1940s.

Above: This piece of sculpture of 1945, entitled 'Construction 12145', demonstrates Sottsass' debt to Rationalism in its use of the rectilinear grid and the juxtaposition of space and mass. Pieces such as this served as models for early ventures into furniture and interior design.

SOTTSASS ASSOCIATI

SOTTSASS ASSOCIATI

Above: This interior, designed in Turin in 1946, is described as 'An Interior for a Young Girl'. It shows how Sottsass transferred his ideas about form and space from sculpture into the environment, and contains in embryo many of his ideas about interior decoration.
Left: This chair was designed by Sottsass for the Triennale of 1947. It combines a geometrical structure with organic features.

SOTTSASS ASSOCIATI

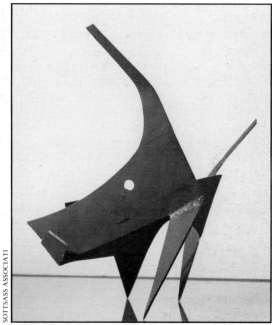

SOTTSASS ASSOCIATI

Above, left and right: Sottsass moved away from the rectilinear grid when he went to Milan in 1946. He experimented instead with a freer kind of abstract composition, in which he either mixed together metal rods and solids as the Constructivist sculptors had, or combined irregular shapes of welded metal in the style of the Surrealists Alexander Calder and Jean Arp. Constructions 08846 and 091647 reflect this injection of dynamism into his work.
Right: This exhibition stand, designed for the Grassotti company in 1948, emphasises Sottsass' debt to Surrealist sculpture.

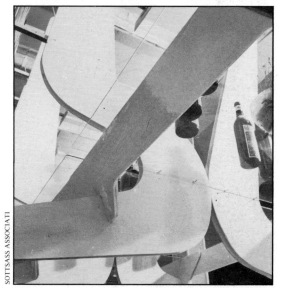

SOTTSASS ASSOCIATI

Sottsass used his experiments with colour, form and space as starting points for his early incursions into design, notably interiors, furniture and household objects; textures, colours and organic forms abound in the interiors from this period. Old is combined with new in an example of 1953. The whole setting is held together visually by subtle lighting from a standard lamp which itself plays a prominent part in the composition. In an apartment in Turin of the same year, colour and potted plants serve as natural partitions differentiating areas: the chairs, designed by Sottsass himself, are a good example of the combination of moulded plastics seat and narrow steel rod legs that Charles Eames had introduced in the late 1940s. Variety is the keynote of these and other interiors, where both natural and synthetic materials find a place. The emphasis is firmly upon the sensorial reality of the surfaces and materials used, rather than on an idealised mathematical definition of space such as the Neo-Plasticists had evolved in the first half of the century.

The dynamism created by the juxtaposition of two- and three-dimensional design invigorates much of Sottsass' work: the integration of surface patterns and paintings into an interior space provides him with an important challenge. He used decorated surfaces both to humanise and to enrich his interiors. This is nowhere more evident than in an interior of 1955 into which paintings by contemporary Italian artists were introduced. The plainness of the interior provided a strong contrast to the works, which were large Gestural paintings. Sottsass

DOMUS FOTO-STUDIO CASALI

In the mid-1950s Sottsass designed interiors for wealthy Milanese clients. In this example from 1953 for Signor Ghedini, Sottsass explores the decorative effects of plants and pictures.

constantly returns to this kind of dialectic, setting rational forms against freer romantic images. He seeks, by combining them, to create a synthesis that gives a more complete approach to design than that provided by the early twentieth-century Functionalists.

Designs for mass-produced objects began to assume a fundamental importance in these years, as they provided an opportunity for combining Sottsass' aesthetic, technical and social interests. It is in this area that he began to consolidate his attempts to overthrow the ghost of Functionalism and return to the richness of traditional craft, to organic design styles such as Art Nouveau, and to react to stimuli from contemporary painting and sculpture.

Plywood, metal sheet and rod provided Sottsass with the possibility of transferring the aesthetic he had learnt from sculptors to functional domestic objects. He designed sets of chairs, lights and vase holders that resembled the constructions of his earlier years and evolved a simple technique of curving sheets of plywood and aluminium by cutting into them and overlapping the raw edges – a trick learnt by most schoolchildren with paper. The plastics firm Kartell experimented with the industrial application of this principle in the mid-1950s, mass producing some of these designs. Sottsass continued to experiment with new ways of making three dimensions out of two. In an article in *Domus* in 1953 he showed how canvas tents, when stretched over their frames, create organic shapes by the simplest of means. The contrast of the undulating canvas surfaces and the straight poles and ropes is echoed in the play between the seat and the metal rod legs of a stool designed in 1954.

The three-dimensional forms produced by Sottsass for the mass-produced goods of this period were characterised by their organic quality and their asymmetry. This is clearly

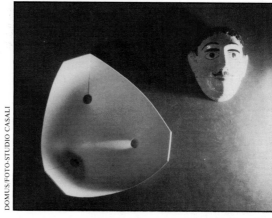

DOMUS/FOTO-STUDIO CASALI

Sottsass evolved a simple technique of turning two-dimensional pieces of paper, plywood and metal into three dimensions merely by making cuts in them. He designed a set of bowls in this way in 1955.

shown in a series of ceramic tableware designed in 1954 in collaboration with Bepi Fiori, which was described in *Domus* as conveying 'the taste of an ancient civilisation interpreted with the feeling of modern sculpture'.[7] This moulded ware was the first of Sottsass' many incursions into ceramics; it was to provide him with one of his favourite materials because of its traditional associations and he was to work simultaneously on mass-produced and handmade ceramics for many years to come.

In the field of small decorative objects – such as some acrylic vases with metal rod holders – and two-dimensional designs for carpets and tapestries, Sottsass employed strong forms and patterns, borrowing from the Constructivist sculptors and the Gestural painters. In a design for the interior of a carpet shop in Turin the full expressive potential of his two- and three-dimensional work combined to create a rich atmosphere in a commercial setting.

Top left: In 1954 Sottsass designed a set of simple ceramic tableware for mass production in response to a commission from Raymor's in New York.
Centre left: These sketches for ceramic designs made in 1955 look ahead to the large ceramic sculptures of the late 1960s.
Below: By the mid-1950s, Sottsass had developed his sculptural interest in metal rod into designs for functional objects – from furniture to vases. This vase of 1952 combines a dynamic use of steel rod with an acrylic bowl.
Bottom: This design for a carpet of 1955 shows Sottsass moving away from pre-war aesthetic principles towards a concern with ideographic signs that was to preoccupy him in the early 1960s – an early instance of his interest in the symbolic meaning of objects.

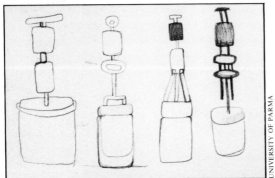

One design stands out as a sign of things to come. The sketch for a telephone of 1954 is the only sortie outside architecture and the applied arts into the realm of industrial design. Yet another exercise in modern sculptural form, it proposes a new unified form for an object that had previously been an amalgam of component parts: this early styling exercise was soon to be joined by the work that Sottsass was to undertake in the following decade for the Olivetti company.

It was in the immediate post-war decade that Sottsass explored most thoroughly his commitment to architecture. The opportunity to become involved in architectural projects arose from the INA-CASA scheme, which was part of the Marshall Plan for the reconstruction of Savona and Novara in northern Italy. Funds were extremely limited and the restraints upon the designs very stringent. Sottsass approached the task without preconceptions, attempting to find a solution to architectural problems in the same *tabula rasa* manner in which he had approached two- and three-dimensional design. The social function of architecture was a new challenge and Sottsass was quick to see a direct link between aesthetic and social perspectives. Not only should the form be emotive, he maintained, but the organisation of the buildings should encourage community interaction. In working towards a formula that would satisfy these two requirements, he was opposing Functionalism on two counts: aesthetically by using decorative features in his building, and ideologically by referring to traditional concepts in the planning of domestic units. In 1936 Sottsass had read Pagano's book on Italian folk architecture and both during his childhood and later during the war years in Montenegro he had had first-hand experience of rustic, vernacular building types. This was to provide him with an architectural vocabulary.

Sottsass began experimenting with architecture in 1947 with this church for the QT8 competition.

In 1947 Sottsass designed a house for the QT8 competition which was essentially neo-Rationalist, but in 1948 he began his work for INA-CASA with a completely different approach. He started by taking photographs of Sardinia where one of his first projects was to be built. (The photographs were later displayed at the 1951 Triennale.) By doing this he could work from a direct knowledge of the environment, rather than from preconceived ideas about building types, and so arrive at a form that was appropriate to its setting.

The first project, which was to be built at Romentina in Novara, was published in *Domus* in 1952 and demonstrated Sottsass' principles at work. The text explained that the laws governing architectural construction are natural ones that must take account of the lie of the land: the longitudinal axis must run from north-west to south-east and the living rooms must face south-west. The models for these workers' houses were rural dwellings of the western Po Valley. The dominant line of the construction is

Below and bottom: From 1948 Sottsass took part in the INA-CASA project, established to reconstruct Savona and Novara. Among his projects was this block of workers' dwellings at Romentino, designed in 1951. The emphasis is on an aesthetic treatment of architectural details and a relationship with the terrain.

SOTTSASS ASSOCIATI

UNIVERSITY OF PARMA

Below: In his housing scheme at Meina of 1951, Sottsass confronted the problem of communal architecture that has presented itself to so many architects through this century.
Bottom: Sottsass' design for a housing scheme at Arborea of 1953 incorporated a coloured ceramic grille by Andrea Cascella.

a dynamic diagonal with open staircases and balconies providing both functional and visual features. Sottsass had succeeded in adding to Le Corbusier's basic principles of simple dwelling units an organic relationship with the terrain and a dynamic aesthetic.

In another project – in Arborea in Sardinia in 1953 – Sottsass laid more emphasis upon decoration by incorporating into the design a colour ceramic grill made by Andrea Cascella that cast moving shadows on the whitewashed walls of the building. The following year, in a project in Gozzano in Novara, he emphasised the communal aspect of the flats by the deliberate inclusion of traditional Italian features such as the piazza and other communal areas that encourage flexible social relationships in a different way from that provided either in the Garden City concept or in Le Corbusier's 'Machine for Living in', the two dominant twentieth-century solutions to the problem of communal architecture. The next year, in the design for housing at Meina, he extended this traditional emphasis by incorporating a large, communal staircase and balconies on which to hang washing.

During these years Sottsass also produced sketches for luxury villas of a more idealised nature, experimenting with the formal and technical aspects of architectural construction. In such projects his main preoccupation was with the expressive potential of huge, curved concrete vaults, reminiscent of shapes employed by Eero Saarinen in his TWA terminal at John F. Kennedy Airport. A villa designed for a site near Lerici owes much to the experience Sottsass gained from working with the sculptor Antoine Pevsner, and exemplifies the aesthetic which runs through much of his work in this period. *Domus* described the designer's concerns: 'In the studio of Sottsass we found more traces of research in this field . . . than is customary in an architect's office. He spends a large part of his time in this type of research which is not, quite often, directly related to practical architectural problems.'6

The last architectural project of this decade was for a school in Siliqua on which Sottsass worked with his father. Once again the natural environment, the climate and the indigenous buildings suggested the architectural solution. The traditional Mediterranean patio featured strongly in the design, and the overall plan which resembled a small village with corridors acting as narrow streets was a familiar one to local people. The bright colours – predominantly blue and yellow, like a Van Gogh painting – were highly appropriate in the strong Mediterranean sunlight. Textured surfaces and plants decorated this otherwise simple structure.

By the mid-1950s Sottsass had ventured along many of the paths that were to determine his subsequent career, but the liberation from Functionalism stands out above all else. He had succeeded in introducing into design the full colour spectrum with all its psychological implications as well as organic forms and tactile surfaces. In addition to this aesthetic experimentation he had also asked some fundamental questions about the relationship between designed objects – be they houses or chairs – and people, discovering that factors such as tradition play as much a part in the communication process as the immediacy of colour and form. This kind of realisation took Sottsass beyond the level of superficial aesthetics and into a deeper investigation of the meaning of objects in the environment.

Sottsass' impact on Italian design in the decade following the war was considerable. Nearly all his architecture and design projects were documented in *Domus* and he participated in the Triennales of 1947, 1951 and 1954. His work for the INA-CASA scheme was recognised as making many important breakthroughs at a time when Italian architecture was receiving attention internationally through the Neo-Liberty movement and publications such as Zevi's *Organic Architecture:* (the Neo-Liberty movement was characterised by a revised use on the part of a number of young Italian architects of some of the organic, expressive shapes used by the Art Nouveau architects and designers at the turn of the century). Sottsass remained outside these movements as he mistrusted anything academic, but in his own intuitive way he was reaching some of the same conclusions.

The decade after the war was one in which Sottsass rejected intellectualism in coming to terms with his own creativity. The designs were experiments first and foremost and very few were put into mass production. By 1955, however, the year in which he was commissioned to do some work for a New York firm, he was ready to design confidently for serial production and to move more definitely away from architecture towards designing a whole range of products that make up the everyday environment.

Consumerism and Style

During the late 1950s and the early 1960s in Italy the term 'design' took on a special significance, both for the recently established manufacturer and for the consumer with his new-found wealth; at the same time a new professional was created – the industrial designer. In no other country, except perhaps in the United States of America where commerce dictated everything, was design considered as so distinct a concept with so much thought and energetic attention directed towards it.

In visual terms a language of industrially produced form emerged in Italy: it combined the familiar American idiom of streamlining with the more purist, sculptural interests of contemporary Scandinavian craftsmen. The result was a sophisticated, highly styled aesthetic which accurately mirrored the cultural aspirations of the Italian middle-class consumer of this epoch.

The years 1955–1965 mark a hiatus between the energetic but often confused experiments of the immediate post-war years and the rejection of design, with its accompanying alternative proposals, that were to characterise Italian design by the middle of the 1960s. It is a forward-looking period, notable for its mood of confidence and brave experimentation. It is also one in which most of the heroic figures of Italian design emerged, willing to forget the past and to put their hopes in a new, prosperous environment for the future.

There were several channels through which these men communicated their messages to the world. These included the Milan Triennales which put an official stamp upon design activities of the period; the Associazione per il Disegno Industriale (the Association of Industrial Design), which was established in 1956 to provide a support system for the professional industrial designer; and the annual design competition, the Golden Compass (*Compasso d'Oro*, established in 1958 under the sponsorship of the well known chain of stores, La Rinascente), which selected the best designs of each year.

In his survey of Italian design in this period Vittorio Gregotti commented that these institutions were unaware of the ideological discussion that lay beneath the surface of production and consumption at this time, and that they tended to stress only the aesthetic of isolated products emphasising their 'techno-functionalism'. This is undoubtedly true and highlights the prevailing attitude of this period – that is, that the perfect design solution was considered in terms of absolute beauty rather than in terms of its social implications.

The extent to which aesthetics dominated both production and consumption in these years was demonstrated by the objects selected for the Eleventh Triennale which took place in 1957. One section of the exhibition was devoted to the 'Production of Art and Industrial Design': it aimed to articulate a number of themes, including the analysis of objects, the 'designer', technique and form, the artist, economics and the consumer. What in fact emerged most strongly was the striking, sculptural appearance of the industrial objects displayed there. Selected by Gillo Dorfles, Leonardo Ricci, Alberto Rosselli and Marco Zanuso, these included a motor bike with a streamlined petrol tank, an asymmetrical, sculptured soda syphon designed by Sergio Asti for Saccab, a plastic bucket with a sensuously curved lid designed by Gino Columbini for Kartell – one of the first examples of the sculptured, plastics moulded functional objects that were soon to become so familiar, and a streamlined television receiver designed for Phonola.

In the designers' section well known names such as Ponti and Nizzoli were singled out for individual attention – the latter's sewing

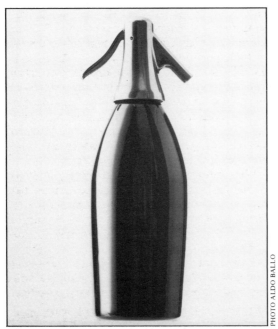

PHOTO ALDO BALLO

CENTRO DOCUMENTAZIONE DOMUS

CENTRO DOCUMENTAZIONE DOMUS

CENTRO DOCUMENTAZIONE DOMUS

Top left: Sergio Asti's soda syphon was designed for Saccab in 1956.
Below left: Kartell was first to exploit the sculptural look in plastic household objects. Colombini's designs were executed in 1956–7.
Top: Berizzi, Butte and Montagni designed this organic tv cabinet for Phonola in 1956.
Above: Nizzoli's 'Mirella' sewing machine for Necchi is an outstanding design of the late 1950s.

Below: The Castiglioni brothers produced their 'Spalter' vacuum cleaner in the late 1950s.
Bottom: Vico Magistretti's table lamp for Artemide was produced in 1965.
Below right: Roberto Menghi's chair, manufactured by the Zanotta furniture company, combines tradition and innovation in its adaptation of the well known safari chair.

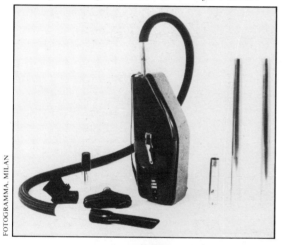

FOTOGRAMMA, MILAN

machine for Necchi, the 'Mirella', was given pride of place as being representative of the vocabulary of industrial form that was emerging in Italy. The subtle curves of the casing on this machine are justified in functional terms as they echo the shape of the electric motor, which is entirely incorporated in the arm. Similarly, the curved asymmetry of the nylon body of the Castiglioni brothers' organically shaped vacuum cleaner, the 'Spalter', which was also exhibited, echoes the machinery inside.

The innovations in industrial design exhibited at the 1957 Triennale were paralleled by the startling shapes and brave experimentation with new materials visible in many of the furniture designs of the period. They were designed by the same ex-architects who had plunged so enthusiastically into other areas of industrial production. Many chairs and tables were now being mass produced and firms such as Arflex,

PHOTO ALDO BALLO

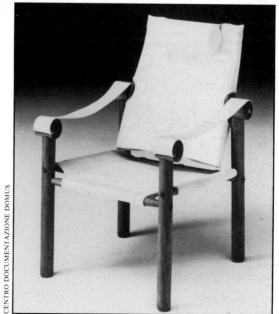

CENTRO DOCUMENTAZIONE DOMUS

CENTRO DOCUMENTAZIONE DOMUS

Below: Among the Italian 'super-designers' of the decade 1955–65, Joe Colombo went further than anyone in his development of an elegant furniture aesthetic. The 'Spider' lamp and the 'Elda' armchair typify his visual style.

ARAM DESIGNS LTD

O-LUCE ITALIA

COMFORT

Top: Zanuso's chair designs for Arflex became increasingly sophisticated in these years.
Above: The Castiglioni brothers' 'Arco' floor lamp of 1962 became a symbol of Italian taste and style in the 1960s.

Gavina, Tecno and Cassina led the field. Significant designs included a chair by Carlo di Carli of 1957 – a sculptured foam body on steel legs, an office chair with a pedestal base designed by Rosselli in 1958, and other designs by Menghi and Nizzoli from the late 1950s which combined the use of new materials with an interest in sculptural form.

The gap between furniture and product design was gradually closing as the same individuals applied their creative imaginations to anything that provided a challenge and could be put into direct production. Firms were quick to exploit this eagerness and employed the new designers on a freelance, consultative basis to style their products for them and imbue them with an 'artistic' quality.

Examples of collaboration between designers and firms that manufactured goods for the home include the work of Nizzoli for the Necchi company between 1953 and 1967, the designs by the Castiglioni brothers for Flos, Kartell, Gavina and Phonola, and the work of Marco Zanuso for Arflex and Borletti. In his experiments in furniture design for Arflex, Zanuso typically manifests the deep commitment that these individuals felt towards their search for formal beauty. He describes his sources and the attention to the manipulation of form in the design for a chair:

Examples of the form we adopted are legion in the vegetable and animal worlds. Many leaves, especially those of tropical plants, are a planar development of the stem, with a 'U' section similar to that hypothesised for the chair. Subsequently the legs reverted to their original shape and we introduced a curvilinear connective element which partially enveloped the legs, providing a box-like structure.[8]

This was the heroic period of Italian design in which the designers saw no limits to the technical and aesthetic possibilities open to them, and plunged headlong into a search for beauty. The experiments became more audacious by the early 1960s and the pages of *Domus* from these years reflected the eminently sculptural concerns of most of the 'artists' working with industry.

Lighting, with its formal freedom and atmospheric possibilities, provided an important focus for many designers; it became a symbol of the aesthetic freedom that they all enjoyed. Sarfatti's lamp for Arteluce displayed at the 1957 Triennale recalls the tall sculptures of Giacometti, and the Castiglioni brothers' famous lamp which seems to hover over a whole interior became a cult object symbolising luxury and good taste – the two qualities that were in great evidence in the early 1960s in Italian middle-class homes.

The 1964 Triennale was entitled 'Leisure', bringing into the open the elitist implications of Italian design in this period. The years of hardship following the war had by now been forgotten and replaced by a period of financial security and an emphasis on the good life. Ponti had written in his first edition of *Domus* in 1948: 'Our ideal of the good life and a level of taste and thought expressed by our homes and manner of living are all part of the same thing and one also with our method of production.'[9] By the mid-1960s his ideal had been fully realised.

If a single figure can be said to epitomise the aesthetic concerns of Italian design in the early 1960s, it is Joe Colombo: he refined his visual language to such an extreme position that the furniture and objects he produced – among them the 'Spider' lamp, the 'Rol' chair and the 'Elda' armchair – are essays in abstract sculpture exerting their aesthetic impact on to the space around them.

Colombo justified his pieces, however, not in terms of their formal properties but in terms of their meaning. He wrote: 'I don't think of myself as an artist, nor as a technician, but as an epistemologist.'[10]

This realisation heralds the presence of a theme which parallels the interest in form of this period. An interest in the semantic or linguistic content of objects emerges from the works of many of the design critics writing in this period. By the mid-1960s it had gathered strength and was evident in articles in *Casabella* by, among others, Gillo Dorfles and Umberto Eco who began to question the validity of defining isolated objects solely in terms of aesthetics and technics and ignoring their role in relation to other objects and to society. A report presented on the occasion of the exhibition 'New Designs for Italian Furniture' explains their radical position questioning the social role of objects: 'The myth of the object as a secondary phenomenon of the fetishism of goods is a true characteristic of our times and its activism.'[11]

This 'critical reversal', as Emilio Ambasz calls it, became increasingly widespread and by the middle of the decade occupied a central position. Many designers who had confidently supported Ponti's ideal of the good life began to think that there was a deeper role for design in society and to question its one-dimensional function. It is within this context that Ettore Sottsass designed his set of furniture for Poltronova in 1965: in so doing he initiated the movement called Anti-Design which provided a focus for designers in the second half of the 1960s.

Ettore Sottsass Jnr: Industrial Designer

'A so-called industrial designer must be put in a position where he is able to play his role to the end, he must find space for discussing the problem of the figure, the iconographic catalogue, the problem of signs, of linguistic destinies.'

E. Sottsass Jnr

The decade 1955 to 1965 witnessed Sottsass' continued and accelerated search for a design language that would communicate on the level of the senses rather than the intellect. Voyages abroad, westwards to the United States in 1956 and 1962, and eastwards to India and the Orient in 1961, presented him with examples of man living in direct contact with his senses, free from what he called 'European anxiety'. These journeys were highly liberating, permitting the young designer to distance himself from his background and to realise that other cultures define their relationships with objects differently from his European Rationalist heritage.

An important new experience for Sottsass in this second phase of his career was his collaboration with the Olivetti company, as a consultant designer for their electronic equipment. This developed, after 1958, into a major facet of his work, replacing his commitment to architecture. It encouraged him to develop a theory of the meaning of industrially produced objects, relevant now to people at work as well as at home.

A third event in this period which had a strong influence on the direction of Sottsass' creative development was of a more personal nature. This was a severe kidney illness that he suffered in 1962, which radically affected his view of the world, causing him to intensify his thoughts about the power of objects as conveyors of human feelings.

The important emphasis of this phase of Sottsass' career is the search for form, not for the isolated object, but for objects that interact with each other in the environment. Form was no longer seen as an end in itself, but took on a quasi-religious significance, standing for an inner reality that had implications for the

'spirit'. The objects produced in this decade begin to display a monumentality which forces their presence on to the spaces and human life around them; in this process they communicate magical values.

This new approach towards the object was born of Sottsass' experience of America. In 1955 he had been commissioned by the New York firm, Raymor, to produce some designs. Raymor had been founded by Irving Richard in 1940 and had a policy of sponsoring modern design; it sold work by contemporary American and Scandinavian designers, including George Nelson and Hans Wegner. Sottsass designed some aluminium vases for them which were produced by the Italian manufacturer Rinnovel.

SOTTSASS ASSOCIATI

Sottsass designed this aluminium vase in 1955.

It was in connection with this commission that Sottsass made his first trip to America. He stayed for several months and worked in George Nelson's office for part of that time. It was while in Nelson's office that he became aware that American culture functions on the level of pure sensation and that the mass-produced object and the mass media serve to provide instant values. Rather than rejecting this as superficial, he entered body and soul into the immediacy of American culture, enjoying – like the Pop artists whom he was soon to admire so much – the impact of the vivid colour and the sensations that emerged, for example, from the pages of *Playboy* magazine as read by his colleagues in Nelson's office.

On his return from the States, Sottsass picked up where he had left off, continuing to design interiors and furnishings for private clients and firms in Milan. Quite suddenly a new shape began to dominate his designs – the rectilinear grid began to take over from the biomorphic forms and patterns of previous years. The display stands for the room of Italian glass at the Eleventh Triennale of 1957 epitomise this new direction, made up as they are of criss-crossed horizontal and vertical pieces of wood. They recall the screens in a Japanese interior and are another attempt by Sottsass to evolve a basic vocabulary of form that will communicate instantly and on its own terms. The mirror frames, table-tops, chair backs, shelving systems and so on that share this grid, either as a structural element or as a surface motif, operate in much the same way as designs by Charles Rennie Mackintosh and Josef Hoffman produced at the turn of the century. Their impact lies in the strength and immediacy of their monumental form rather than in a complex analysis of that form.

Opposite: Sottsass designed the room of Italian glass at the Triennale of 1957.
Below: In the late 1950s Sottsass designed a series of furniture for Poltronova consisting of mirrors, tables, chairs and shelving systems.
Right: These enamelled dishes of 1958 show Sottsass' interest in ideographic signs.

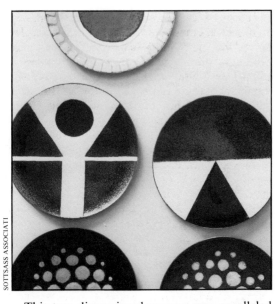

In keeping with this search for a new aesthetic alphabet, Sottsass developed in the same years an interest in ideographic signs – always hand drawn – which covered the surfaces of many designs of the period. Inspired by the automatic sign-writing of the American Abstract Expressionist painters (those artists including Arshile Gorky and Jackson Pollock who in New York in the 1950s covered huge untreated canvases with blobs and drips of paint in a way that expressed their inner subconscious compulsions), Sottsass let his hand take over, creating a set of abstract marks – near-circles, stripes, blobs, dots, rough grids – which, like doodles, take on an identity of their own. He developed, in this way, a sign-system that decorated the surfaces of many of his objects – trays, ceramics, furniture, fabrics – bestowing on them a significance that is essentially sensorial and unrelated to the objects' primary function. It was a way also of linking objects to each other without reference to their use.

This two-dimensional concern was paralleled by Sottsass' determination to work with the spatial properties of colour. In a number of interiors executed in the late 1950s he experimented with colour as a spatial element, using it to decorate the floor, wall and other surfaces, and treating them as elements in a composition, juxtaposed with other features such as furniture, plants and ceramic ornaments. In an interior of 1957 described in *Domus* as 'a composition of walls', the atmosphere is created by a number of large Gestural paintings produced by a group of artists who were interested in the effect of paintings not in a frame, but in total space. In a similar interior of 1959 wooden partitions and cabinets are used to separate the living areas and much is made of graphic and chromatic detail on all the two-dimensional surfaces. A writer in *Domus* describes this arrangement as 'an attitude linked with modern painting'.[12] A later project, the Gughelmone bar designed in 1962, was designed as an environment in which the public would stay a few minutes, have a cup of coffee and go. Sottsass surrounded the space with large photo-murals of subjects that would appeal to the clientele expected to frequent the bar – 'men, some sports fans and some modern girls'.[13] He then juxtaposed these two-dimensional images with a grid ceiling and brightly coloured moulded plastics seats. Another interior in which the wall surfaces played an important part in the totality of the composition was the one Sottsass designed for his Chinese friend, Tchou, in Milan. Atmosphere is once again of prime importance and the design reflects the oriental heritage of the client. Bright colours – reds, oranges and purples – abound on the walls, creating strong spatial effects and setting off the floor of yellow mosaic marble.

Sottsass continued to approach the problem of design as a fine artist, transferring the discoveries of contemporary painters and sculptors into design. In America he came across the work of many artists who were trying to exchange illusory space for real space by using colour on the surface of the canvas. He echoed many of their discoveries in interior compositions and, in his smaller decorative objects, which constitute important elements in those interiors, continued to develop the ideographic language that he had evolved through the late 1950s. Among these were enamelled plates, plastic-laminated objects, lampshades and ceramics.

UNIVERSITY OF PARMA

SOTTSASS ASSOCIATI FOTO-STUDIO CASALI

SOTTSASS ASSOCIATI

Above left: Sottsass' sketch for an interior of 1957 shows his interest in surface pattern.
Below left: In this interior for Via Cappuccio of 1959, Sottsass plays with plants and paintings.
Above: In 1962 Sottsass designed an interior for the Gughelmone bar in Milan.
Opposite: In 1963 Sottsass designed an interior for Tchou – a much loved colleague at Olivetti.

The manipulation of clay took on for Sottsass, in this period, an importance that was to remain constant throughout his later career. He was interested in finding a medium that straddled traditional and contemporary problems and in concerning himself with objects that had an established position as tools in society. Sottsass wanted to avoid the production of objects as status symbols, and he considered that ceramics had a more fundamental relationship with their user by virtue of their original use in primitive societies in which human and cosmic laws were closely intertwined.

Sottsass' first foray into ceramics was as part of the commission for Raymor's. With the help of Aldo Landi, the art director of the Bitossi factory at Montelupo near Florence, he began experiments with terracotta, a traditional Italian material. The indigenous nature of this clay implied for Sottsass that it was naturally integrated into everyday Italian life and culture and not, like Eastern ceramics, tied up with religious thought. He wrote on this subject: 'I think it was always kept in a popular area of non-religious gestures, in the area of cardboard theatre rather than in the area of the temple.'[14]

A series of ceramic pots and vases produced in 1957 display the same simple shapes and are decorated with the same simple patterns as traditional rustic Mediterranean ware. Their unpretentiousness is in marked contrast to the precious craft products from the Scandinavian countries that were flooding the market in those

years. The following year Sottsass incorporated ceramics with wood and metal in some designs for mirror frames, and produced another series of ceramics with Bitossi. They display the same characteristic marks as the designs from the previous year, but are more sophisticated and adventurous in the sculptural quality of their form and the texture of their surfaces. In 1959 another series appeared from the Bitossi factory, this time decorated with highly stylised geometric patterns in black, white, yellow and turquoise. The differences between these ceramic objects and other elements of the interiors – chests, tables, mirrors – were gradually disappearing and by the end of the 1950s Sottsass' ceramics had become just one element in his interior compositions.

Following his trip to India in 1961 – after which Sottsass wrote, 'we could never be entirely the same' – and the illness that he suffered the following year, he changed direction significantly. In 1963 he produced his first set of ceramics that have explicitly mystical associations. Entitled 'The Ceramics of Darkness', the set was exhibited at the Galleria del Sestante in Milan, and consisted of 70 pieces, all of which are variations on the cylinder. They are characterised by the sombreness of their colours and the new mandala-like shapes on their surfaces. Sottsass claimed that they acted as a kind of exorcism, serving to bring him back from his encounter with darkness, and that by producing them he was not marketing ceramics but was 'raising the object to a level of concentration so as to release it from its lesser functions and place it within a higher cultural sphere'.[15]

A year later Sottsass celebrated his return to health and vitality by dedicating a new series of ceramics to the Indian goddess Shiva, the symbol of life. This was his first conscious attempt to create a set of objects that functioned as 'spiritual diagrams'. These ceramics are covered with dots, circles and other shapes vaguely reminiscent of the patterns on Indian drawings of cosmic rhythms; Sottsass described them as an example of 'design as memorandum for the mental and psychic operations necessary for liberation'.[16] He saw them as uniting object and user through 'gestures', by which he meant that the objects should reflect back on the user and make him increasingly aware of his own position, rather than impose their own future on him. The objects are photographed in natural surroundings rather than in an interior to minimise the direct functional relationship between object and user and to maximise the spiritual relationship between them.

Sottsass produced relatively few objects in the early 1960s. The period was dominated instead by the voyages that he took with his wife Nanda to the east and to the west. The fusion of these two differing experiences is captured in a series of paintings that he produced in 1963 and 1964. The content is oriental in origin with an

SOTTSASS ASSOCIATI/FOTO-STUDIO CASALI

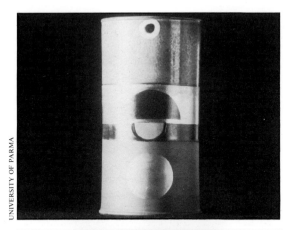

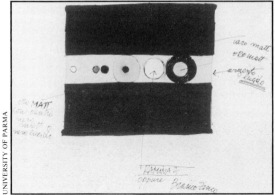

Opposite: Sottsass applied the same ideographic signs to the surfaces of his ceramic objects as he did to so many other of his designs from this period. These vases were produced in 1958–9.
Left, top and centre: The series entitled 'The Ceramics of Darkness' was produced after an illness in 1963 and exhibited in Milan. Abstract patterns resembling mandalas decorate the surfaces of these sombre objects.
Bottom left: The following series – 'The Ceramics to Shiva' of 1964 – represented Sottsass' symbolic return to life. He called them 'spiritual diagrams', covering their surfaces with abstract shapes.
Below: In the early 1960s Sottsass spent much time painting. Like the work of the second generation of American Abstract Expressionists, he worked with sets of abstract signs.

UNIVERSITY OF PARMA

UNIVERSITY OF PARMA

SOTTSASS ASSOCIATI

SOTTSASS ASSOCIATI

abundance of mandalas and other similar geometric motifs, but the way the images are displayed on the canvas recalls the work of contemporary American painters, especially Frank Stella, Ad Reinhardt and other members of the Hard-Edge Abstractionist school – a school which, coming after the expressive forms of the Abstract Expressionists, reinstated a sense of geometric order into their large abstract colour compositions of the early 1960s. The title of one of Sottsass' paintings, a brightly coloured work of 1963, 'Marilyn Monroe', links Sottsass firmly with American culture.

Sottsass retained an affinity with avant-garde American painting from Abstract Expressionism in the mid-1950s to Pop Art in the following decade. Not only was this interest reflected in his designs, but he wrote a number of pieces of art criticism for *Domus* in the mid-1960s. In 1963 he wrote at length about Dada, which was being reassessed in America at that time in the light of the emergent Pop Art movement; the following year he wrote two further pieces entitled 'Dada is dead' and 'Pop and non Pop'. The mass media imagery that was inspiring such artists as Warhol, Lichtenstein and Oldenburg appealed strongly to Sottsass, whose commitment to the communicative power of images and objects enabled him to identify closely with the pleasure that these artists gained from Pop culture.

The series of furniture produced for the Milan firm Poltronova in 1965 demonstrated the closeness between Sottsass and contemporary American Pop culture. He wrote about how these non-traditional furniture pieces were inspired:

This group of furniture seems to be the result of an experience I had in California when we went with Nanda and her friends who are Ginsberg, Bob Dylan, Ferlinghetti and the Hell's Angels around all night through the houses of other friends and friends of friends who altogether had thrown the illogicalities and contradictions of the bourgeois, low bourgeois and proletarian consumeristic environment out of the window and had been left with empty rooms, with mattresses on the floor, with letters in cardboard boxes, with the shining refrigerators slashed with the points of scissors and the few pieces of furniture left – old chairs and writing desks collected in the high streets around the garbage cans – had a strange look, as of funereal monuments in the middle of the dirty square of those emptied rooms.[17]

In the furniture he produced after this experience, when he had seen the complete reversal of furniture as status symbol, he attempted to incorporate new meanings and to break totally with convention. The new objects he proposed looked less like shelves than traffic lights, dials and mechanical equipment: he was deliberately drawing on shapes from the repertoire of public sign-systems to provide a level of recognisability, but the pieces also performed a deconditioning function because of the novelty of their forms and uses. There are vague stylistic references to Mackintosh and Art Deco objects of the 1930s.

Sottsass' collaboration with the firm of Olivetti began in 1958 and represented yet another facet of his varied interpretation of the term 'designer'. His involvement with industry in general had expanded in the 1950s with his work for several furniture firms, and it was a natural development that he should jump at the opportunity of working with a firm that was beginning to produce objects that belong very much to the second half of the twentieth century – computers and other electronic equipment. Sottsass had made isolated forays into industrial design – for example the telephone of 1955 – but this was merely consolidating his role as designer, complementing his work as architect and applied artist.

SOTTSASS ASSOCIATI

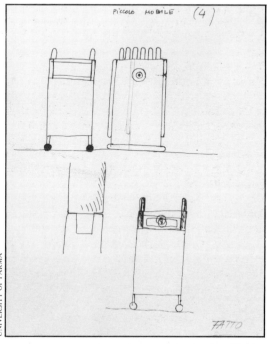

UNIVERSITY OF PARMA

SOTTSASS ASSOCIATI/ALBERTO FIORAVANTI

Above, left and right: In 1965 Sottsass designed a major set of furniture for Poltronova which was influenced by the American Pop painters and signs culled from the mass environment; these pieces of furniture resemble traffic signals and other familiar urban objects.

Left: The Lotus table, designed for Poltronova, introduced the chunky 'Mickey Mouse' look into Sottsass' furniture.

The arrangement that Sottsass agreed with Olivetti was a very special one: he maintained his independence by working as a consultant with a team composed of other consultants and collaborators employed directly by the company. Another special characteristic of his relationship with Olivetti was his contact with the management: Roberto Olivetti, the son of the founder Adriano Olivetti, and Mario Tchou, the technical director, since company policy put design under direct management control. All three men were to become close friends.

Sottsass' first project for Olivetti's new electronics department was a computer called the ELEA 9003. It was a complicated system: the central processor consisted of a series of cabinets in lines and in groups of three; in each group the middle cabinet stayed put and the outside two turned to give access to the cards. Sottsass instigated a few simple innovations in the design that emphasised his commitment to the environmental nature of the machinery. Firstly he lowered the height of the cabinets so that the operators could see each other; and secondly he created a network of aerial cable ducts connecting central processor with the peripheral machines that could grow with the system. From working with the ELEA Sottsass learnt that he needed to develop a standard electronic packaging element, so he began to work on this in 1961 while also undertaking a meticulous programme of ergonomic research

to evolve a group of measurements on a human scale. He wrote characteristically about this systematisation:

Physical rules of this kind do not limit liberty but, on the contrary, open it up . . . The Japanese Tatami is a rule which is at the base of the incredible store of imagination in the Japanese culture and the dimensions of bricks are at the base of the incredible store of imagination in the Mediterranean and European cultures and so on.[18]

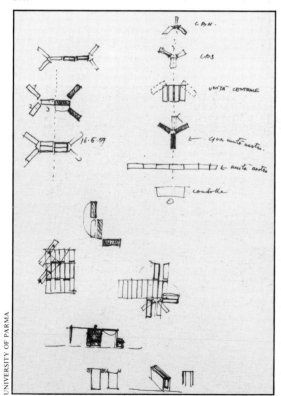

Sottsass' first major project for Olivetti, the ELEA 9003 computer of 1959, represented a radical step forward in computer design, both aesthetically and ergonomically.

In aesthetic terms the ELEA computer moved radically away from the traditional concept of 'steel cupboards along the wall' and became a piece of sculpture that used mass, space and colour as its raw materials. Colour symbolism – the external wall is white with red, and the controls mauve, turquoise and yellow – was used to relate parts to each other and to the whole. Sottsass saw the monolithic forms of the computer providing a unit in the new family of forms that has modified the visual landscape of contemporary society, and felt that as much thought should be given to their aesthetic and symbolic content as to that of a flower-vase or a teacup.

Among other projects that Sottsass undertook for Olivetti during this decade were several designs for typewriters – the Tekne 3 of 1958–60, the Praxis 48 of 1962–3, and the De Luxe and Dora portables of 1965 – and a series of electronic equipment including the RP60 and Mercator 5000 of 1960 and the Logos 27 of 1964. These were all inventive, innovatory designs that took electronic and office machinery outside the normal bounds of efficiency for efficiency's sake and included considerations about its symbolic and psychological functions. The Praxis 48, for example, gave a new identity to the typewriter: with its carriage at the same level as the machine body, it was a small, light, compact electric machine. *Domus* described it as 'almost a toy, a decorative object which can be left on the table'.[19] The precision and regularity in the styling of this and the other objects, combined with the awareness of the human relationship with the machine, puts Olivetti products in a class of their own in this period.

By the middle of the 1960s Sottsass had reached maturity as a designer. His travels and his researches into the meanings of objects within their social context, together with his

ALBERTO FIORAVANTI

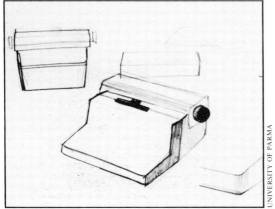

UNIVERSITY OF PARMA

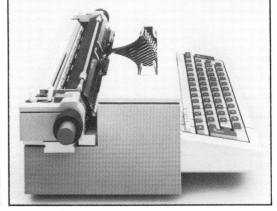

Opposite, top and bottom left: The Tekne 3 was Sottsass' first electric typewriter for Olivetti. Designed in 1958–60, it typifies his concern for visual regularity and attention to detail. Opposite, bottom right: Designed in 1962–3, the Praxis 48 took typewriter shell design one step further in the direction of pure form.

Below: The Lettera De Luxe typewriter, designed by Sottsass in 1965, extended Marcello Nizzoli's original conception of the early 1950s into a more stylised, sophisticated portable typewriter.

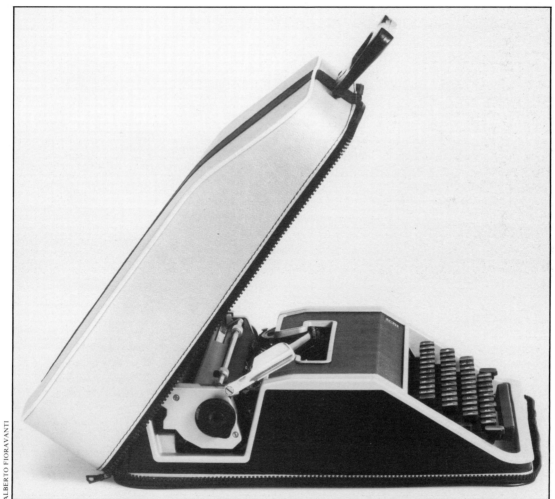

ALBERTO FIORAVANTI

rigorous investigations into the raw material of design – form, space, colour and so on – had combined to provide him with a solid background from which to take on work in many different design fields. In this second decade of his career industrial design has usurped the position that architecture had held in the previous ten years. (He did, however, complete one project for a house at the seaside in 1962 which reflected his prevailing interest in eastern religion, as it contained a small garden that was dedicated to meditation.)

The forays into mysticism and Pop Art were symptoms of a deeper concern – a search for a design philosophy rooted in human values. They were part of the desire for an alternative to the dehumanised theory of Functionalism that would take intuition and sensitivity as starting points. India and America provided models in which man was once more at the centre of things, appearing to control the objects around him by imbuing them with his consciousness. Sottsass saw this as the way forward, a way of

formulating a new kind of design which spoke a meaningful language to the people for whom it was made. Before this could be achieved the vestiges of Functionalism had to be removed once and for all, and this meant one more concerted attack on the design establishment. The intention of the movement known as Anti-Design in the second half of the 1960s was to deliver the final blow.

Left: Sottsass designed a range of office machinery for Olivetti including computers, read-out equipment and calculators. Logos 27 was designed in 1964.
Top: Sottsass designed the little manual portable typewriter called Dora in 1965.
Above: One of the few architectural projects that Sottsass undertook in this decade was his House at the Seaside of 1962, which incorporated a small garden for meditation.

Radicalism and Anti-Design

'The methodological point of view is connected with the tradition of the Modern Movement, with particular emphasis on Functionalism. In the Italian architectural schools of today this point of view is no longer considered sufficient for an analysis of the reality in which architecture has to function.'
Marco Zanuso

In the late 1960s and the early 1970s the most interesting aspect of Italian design was the rejection of the immediate past on the part of a small group of young architect-designers, who were dissatisfied with the élitist definition of design that had evolved in the previous decade. While the established companies and major figures of Italian design continued to evolve even more sophisticated, beautiful and luxurious objects for middle-class consumption (sustained by the system of exhibitions and sponsorship upon which they depended so heavily and which continued to publicise and mythologise their achievements), a reassessment of design began to emerge. It posed a threat to the foundations upon which design had been built in the post-war period, and attempted a redefinition of its role in society.

This self-doubt was not restricted to design alone, but characterised a period in Western cultural history in which many of the values of society as a whole were being questioned. The student unrest of these years highlighted some of the major doubts and fears felt by the young generation that had inherited the post-war society created by their parents.

This was felt particularly strongly in Italy, and the early signs of malaise about the role of design in the environment were felt in the major architectural schools, first in Florence and subsequently in Milan, Turin and Rome. Described both as 'Counter-Design' and 'Anti-Design', the movement that grew out of these misgivings was characterised by its use of irony and by its utopianism. It turned the development of architecture – and by implication of design – back on itself, developing its disciplines

as a medium for self-criticism. What emerged from this debate was a kind of architecture and design that functioned, not to provide consumable products, but as self-commentary.

A number of distinct tactics were used as means of side-stepping the traps that the previous generation had fallen into. These included a deliberate exploitation of bad taste or kitsch, and of eclecticism as a way out of the formal purism of Functionalism. Much of the Anti-Design produced in this period was self-confessedly nostalgic and made overt visual references to the popular styling of the 1920s and 1930s; often these styles were unashamedly mixed together. Often no objects were actually produced and the architect-designer made use of alternative media in order to express himself. Most commonly, photography and the written word replaced the product as the most accessible means of direct communication.

There were clear alignments between Anti-Design and contemporary movements in the fine arts, particularly Neo-Dada and Conceptual Art or, to use Germano Celant's term, 'Arte Povera'. Here also the intention was to make art that functioned as its own critic and to bypass traditional media and tired artistic conventions. Anti-Design and Anti-Art remained closely interrelated through the second half of the 1960s, as demonstrated by the dependence of designs such as the 'Sacco' by Gatti, Paolini and Teodora of 1969 and the 'Joe Sofa' by Lomazzo, D'Urbino and De Pas of 1970 on the soft sculptures of the American Pop artist Claes Oldenburg, and by the similarity of work by a number of conceptual artists to the projects of Superstudio and Gruppo Strum.

PHOTO ALDO BALLO

PHOTO ALDO BALLO

PHOTO ALDO BALLO

PHOTO ALDO BALLO

In spite of the development of radical design, projects such as Zanuso and Sapper's tv sets for Brionvega, Magistretti's furniture for Cassina and Livio Castiglioni's Artemide lamp maintained the sleek Italian look in the 1960s.

TATE GALLERY

Because one of the premises of Anti-Design was its fundamental rejection of design synonymous with consumption and therefore with the ethic of capitalism, the products of the Anti-Designers were essentially non-commercial and depended upon exhibitions and publication for their dissemination. The magazines IN and *Casabella* devoted themselves to the cause of Anti-Design from the mid-1960s onwards and published articles and designs throughout the period in question. In one such article the new role for the designer who ceases to contribute to the system of producing more to consume more is described:

The designer ... is no longer the artist who helps us to make our homes beautiful, because they will never be beautiful, but the individual who moves on a dialectical as well as formal plane and stimulates behavioural patterns which will contribute to full awareness, which is the sole premise required for a new equilibrium of values and finally for the evolution, or, if you will, the recovery of man himself.[20]

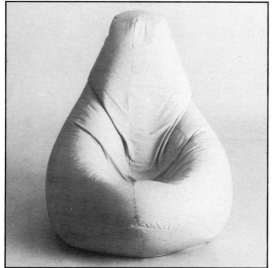

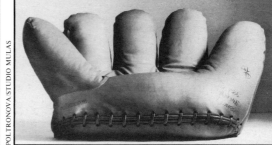

POLTRONOVA/STUDIO MULAS

Above left: American 'soft sculpture' such as Claes Oldenburg's 'Soft Drainpipe' had a strong influence on Italian furniture in the mid-1960s.
Left: Zanotta produced the 'Sacco' chair in the mid-1960s – the ultimate in flexible form.
Above: The 'Joe Sofa', presented at the Salone del Mobile in 1970, owed much to Pop soft sculpture.

The visual source of much of this work derived from the utopian graphic visions of the English architectural group Archigram; for example, 'Plug-in City' of 1964, which employs the imagery of science fiction to envisage a future city in which advanced technology has enabled flexibility and expendability to become the order of the day.

In Italy the first exhibition of Superarchitecture was held in Pistoia in 1966, the same year in which two of the major Anti-Design groups were formed in Florence – Archizoom and Superstudio. The former organised the exhibition in Pistoia and a second one in Modena in 1967. Archizoom was also responsible for the 'Centre for Electric Conspiracy' at the Fourteenth Triennale in 1968 and for another exhibition of radical architecture in 1970 entitled 'No-Stop City'. Their designs have a distinct Dadaistic quality and include 'Dream Beds' of 1967, which are giant, kitsch, fantasy sleep-environments, crammed full of visual references to Art Deco and Pop culture; their close resemblance to altar-pieces emphasises Archizoom's belief in design as essentially ritualistic and anthropocentric.

Superstudio took a more conceptual, intellectual approach towards the question of Anti-Design. The group sought 'to exorcise formal poverty by reaffirming the universal value of the idea of architecture'.[21] Unlike Archizoom, it accepted architecture as a form of representation and produced numerous schemes for architectural projects of 'continuous monuments' and 'ideal cities' that consist of 'networks of energy and communication'. It made frequent reference to an idea that it called 'evasion design', which was used to replace product design. Its work – both two-dimensional projects and three-dimensional designs – was characterised, above all, by the recurrence of a grid used to symbolise anonymity. In 1970, together with Gruppo 9999, it set up the Separate School for Expanded Conceptual Architecture.

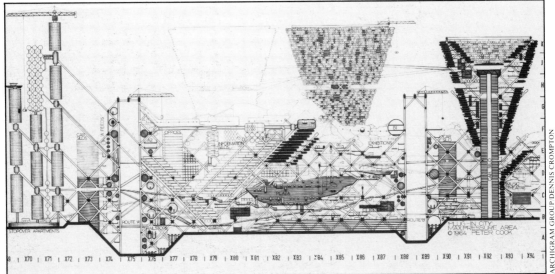

ARCHIGRAM GROUP DENNIS CROMPTON

ARCHIZOOM ASSOCIATI

The English architectural group Archigram had a strong influence upon Italian Radical architecture and design in the late 1960s and early 1970s. Their 'Plug-in City' of 1964 (opposite), for example, inspired projects by Archizoom such as 'No-Stop City' of 1970 (left, top and centre) and others, such as this furniture of 1971 (below) and 'Continuous Monument' of 1969 (bottom), both by Superstudio.

ARCHIZOOM ASSOCIATI

SUPERSTUDIO

SUPERSTUDIO

Gaetano Pesce followed Oldenburg's example in these furniture designs for Cassina. Rejecting the smooth contours of Italian design of the early 1960s, they emphasise comfort rather than form.

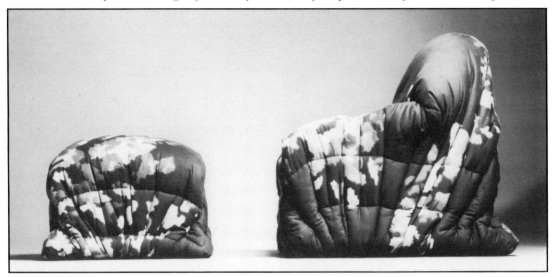

Among other members of the Counter-Design Movement were individuals such as Gaetano Pesce and Ugo La Pietra and groups such as Gruppo Strum and the UFO Group, and a number of lesser known architects and designers who worked within this ambience of radicalism and experimentation.

Gaetano Pesce is a particularly interesting figure as he was working in an area in which he was entirely alone. The objects he produced – among them a giant angled lamp, a huge squashy sofa and a strange bookcase with uneven edges – emphasise the alienation between man and object and the impossibility of communication between them as long as consumption is the sole mediating factor. He uses distortion and exaggeration as 'absurd' devices for commenting upon his observations. Rather than turning to alternative media, Pesce uses the language of design to make its own self-commentary.

In 1973 many of the designers involved in the radical movement – Archizoom, Remo Buti, Ricardo Dalisi, Ugo La Pietra, Gruppo 9999, Pesce, Gianni Pettena, Sottsass, Superstudio, the UFO Group and Zziggurat – met in the offices of *Casabella* to found 'Global Tools', which they described as:

A system of laboratories in Florence dedicated to prompting the study and use of natural technical materials and their relative behavioural characteristics. The object of GLOBAL TOOLS *is to stimulate free development of individual creativity.*[22]

It was seen as an alternative to the training in architecture and design offered at that time in Italy.

The previous year, 1972, had witnessed the first big exhibition of Italian design outside Italy: this was organised by Emilio Ambasz, the curator of design at the Museum of Modern Art in New York, and entitled 'The New Domestic

Landscape'. It was an ambitious exhibition which attempted to show developments in Italian design of the previous ten years as well as to represent contemporary developments. This latter aim was fulfilled by the museum's commissioning many major designers to create a micro-living environment. The brief was very specific and the results showed clearly the main preoccupations of the radical designers and their attempt to move away from the creation of isolated objects towards general environments. All the familiar names in Italian design were represented and the enormous contribution that Italy had made to international design in the post-war period was immediately apparent from the exhibits selected.

What emerged most clearly from the New York exhibition was the unequalled analytical abilities of the Italian designer with reference to the social, economic and cultural context of design. It was this interest in analysing and defining the meaning of objects – rather than simply producing them in an ad hoc manner – that characterised the third phase of the career of Ettore Sottsass Jnr. He, more than any other individual, inspired and encouraged a supremely radical attitude towards design and the environment.

MUSEUM OF MODERN ART, NEW YORK/CENTRO DI

'Italy: The New Domestic Landscape', the exhibition held at the Museum of Modern Art in New York in 1972, provided an opportunity for several designers – among them Joe Colombo – to experiment with flexible environments.

Ettore Sottsass Jnr: Anti-Designer

'The time being over when utensils generated ideas and when ideas generated utensils, now ideas *are* utensils.'

Archigram

During the late 1960s and the early 1970s Sottsass brought many embryonic intuitions, visions and obsessions to fruition, finding ways of expressing them that had not been possible earlier in his career.

The period is characterised by a supreme freedom. Sottsass responded to the dictates of his inner self, never becoming a slave to the industries that he worked with so closely. He continued to create furniture, interiors, ceramics and jewellery developing, as he did so, ideas about the form and language of the objects that constitute an intrinsic part of the human landscape; at the same time he deepened his relationship with the Olivetti company, extending his range to office furniture and office systems in order to study questions about the communication between objects and their users. His final preoccupation during these years was his return to architecture – not to real buildings, but to utopian visions of future cities and environments where all the problems inherent in an urban, mass-consumer society had been removed and man lived once more in touch with his senses and with nature.

The tone of Sottsass' works and writings produced in the years following 1966 is intensely radical. He saw man inhabiting a doomed planet where visual and verbal communication and fulfilled human existence had been made impossible by industry, consumerism and urban life in general.

Sottsass' solution to these problems is not that of the political radical; he functions instead alongside industry, creating objects that aim to 'decondition' man and to encourage meditation and love instead of perpetuating the competitive work ethic of industrial production. In an article in *Domus* in 1970, Sottsass explained his intentions:

I just started to think that if there was any point in designing objects, it was to be found in helping people to live somehow, I mean in helping people to somehow recognise and free themselves, I mean that if there was a point in designing objects, it could only be found in achieving a kind of therapeutic action, handing over to the objects the function of stimulating the perception of one's own adventures.[23]

The desire to create objects that would act as 'catalysts of perception' implies a break with the industrial norm and a return to the individual, contemplative life where fulfilment through self-knowledge and an understanding of the senses are paramount. There are, as has already been suggested, strong mystical undertones in Sottsass' philosophy of life; these come strongly to the fore in this period, expressed in several series of ceramics – among them the 'Tantra' and 'Yantra' series of 1969 and 1970 – which are environmental pieces aimed at stimulating meditation and self-awareness. This strong oriental influence is offset, however, by the appearance of his objects – particularly his furniture and ceramics – which derives from American and European avant-garde painting and sculpture. Through a careful blend of form and content Sottsass succeeds in straddling two very different cultures.

The tactics that he employed in reaching this position were varied and complex. He wrote that he wanted to 'widen the concept of functionalism to the subconscious and unconscious psychic spheres',[24] and to this end he adopted a number of stances that emphasised the non-rational aspects of thought and creativity. He moved from strong affiliations with fine art to an interest in kitsch and popular styling, to mysticism, mythology and symbolism, through to utopian visions complete with images of sexuality and hallucinogenic fantasy. These became metaphors for an anti-Functionalist design and he used them as baselines for his experiments with furniture, ceramics and hardware for Olivetti and for his drawings. Alessandro Mendini has written that Sottsass employed 'destiny, meditation, sign, variation, nature, irony and meta-technique'[25] as devices in his creations. These were only starting-points for an œuvre that touches many facets of the complex interrelationship of man and his environment.

In an interview published in the catalogue to an exhibition of his work in Jerusalem, Sottsass claimed: 'I am searching for ways to help design to acquire basic values, life-values, which will assist it to turn out more than just another chair.'[26]

In 1966 Sottsass designed a series of furniture for the Milan firm Poltronova. He used plastic-laminate for the surfaces of the objects – mainly wardrobes – and bright colours in stripes, thick diagonal lines and other strict geometric patterns. The sources of visual inspiration for these pieces were the vivid colours of the Pop painters, such as Roy Lichtenstein and Andy Warhol, combined with the geometric shapes of a painter such as Frank Stella and the Minimal structures of sculptors such as Sol LeWitt, Don Judd, Robert Morris and Robert Smithson. The works by Sol LeWitt of the early 1960s, entitled variously 'Hanging Structure' (1962), 'Wall Structure' (1962) and 'Hanging Structure (with stripes)' (1963), vividly resemble the abstract shapes and surface patterns that Sottsass evolved in this series of furniture. The impact that American painters and sculptors made upon him during his time in the United States in the early 1960s – especially the work of those people associated with 'Pop' painting, Minimal sculpture and Conceptual Art – is clearly present in his work of that decade.

Below: Sottsass' furniture designed for Poltronova in 1966–7 owes much to American Pop painting and the more geometric work of Frank Stella. Covered with plastic laminate, the pieces resemble monoliths and ziggurats and oppose any preconceived notions of furniture.

Bottom: This wardrobe of 1966 shows Sottsass' debt to American Minimal sculpture. Like the sculptor, he is attempting to create a basic vocabulary of form, reduced to its essentials.

SOTTSASS ASSOCIATI

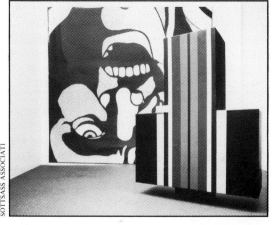

SOTTSASS ASSOCIATI

The formal intention of both LeWitt's and Sottsass' work is to employ a basic vocabulary of form (in this case simple, geometric shapes) in order to renew its linguistic potential; to stimulate fundamental emotional responses in the spectator; and, perhaps most importantly, to act forcefully on the space surrounding the object. The monumentality of both artists' work produces a total spatial experience that works instantly upon anyone who enters the environment of the objects. A commentator in *Domus* wrote of Sottsass' wardrobes:

Isolated in the middle of the room and banded with colours, they eliminate, as it were, the presence of the walls. They make reference to no other wardrobes and exist only in function of the mutual relationship between object and environment.[27]

Sottsass went further than LeWitt, however, in endowing his objects with a specific use, emphasised in the photographs of his furniture by the inclusion of objects in the spaces around the wardrobes – a pair of boots, a tennis racquet and balls – acting as visual clues to signify that the furniture exists to be consumed and that it is this that defines its function and meaning.

The objects are essentially non-assertive, permitting their users total freedom of action, but also – by their altar-like character – encouraging ritualistic behaviour. The names given to the pieces, such as 'Nirvana', confirm their mystical flavour. Sottsass has redefined the nature and role of furniture in terms of its appearance *and* its use, thus providing an alternative tradition for the functional object.

The next major series of furniture appeared in 1970. Visually it had moved away from the earlier series as it made strong use of curved forms and more sensuous lines – what Sottsass himself called 'forms of feminine origin'. Once again the form employed provides the necessary link between maker and consumer, and here

Sottsass makes references to the shapes employed in the styled consumer objects of the 1930s – the so-called 'Hollywood Style' which, by the 1960s, had been subsumed by critics and historians under the category known as kitsch. For Sottsass, kitsch was another escape from Functionalism. It implies extravagance and uselessness – style for style's sake – and as such provides him with another metaphor for non-rational communication between man and objects. The ziggurat shapes of Art Deco remained a constant in Sottsass' formal vocabulary up to the mid-1970s, making an appearance in a whole range of objects including furniture, ceramics and glass.

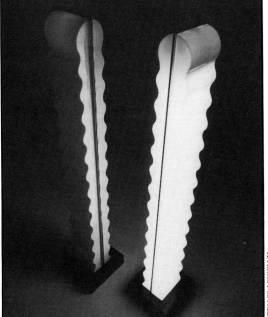

SOTTSASS ASSOCIATI

Above: Sottsass' 'Cometa' lamp of 1970 owes much to American neon sculpture from this period. Opposite: Sottsass' 'grey furniture' of 1970 combines the 'Hollywood Style' with 'Pop'.

Sottsass called this series of furniture (which he intended to be considered as a unified group) – which comprised a huge bed with rounded corners and neon lights, a mirror with a wavy neon frame, a corner cupboard framed by round-cornered fluorescent tubes, a table, a bookcase, a magazine rack and so on – his 'grey furniture', because:

Grey is a very sad colour, maybe the colour which my hairs are going into; I mean a colour that will create some problems for anyone who would like to use it for advertising detergents, toothpaste, vermouth, aperitifs in general, Coca-Cola, elettro-domestici, *deodorants and all that.*[28]

The environmental impact of the furniture was intended to work by suffocation: that is, the inhabitant was surrounded by so much shiny grey plastic that the conventional meaning of 'bourgeois' furniture was inevitably destroyed.

During the 1970s Sottsass continued to produce other individual pieces of furniture such as the 'Mickey Mouse' table for Bonacina in 1972 with its characteristic monolithic quality, the yellow secretary's chair for Olivetti in 1973 and some lights for the German firm Erco, also in 1973; but, increasingly, he moved into total environments, preferring to see living spaces as unified, neutral, flexible areas within which people go about their daily lives. In 1967

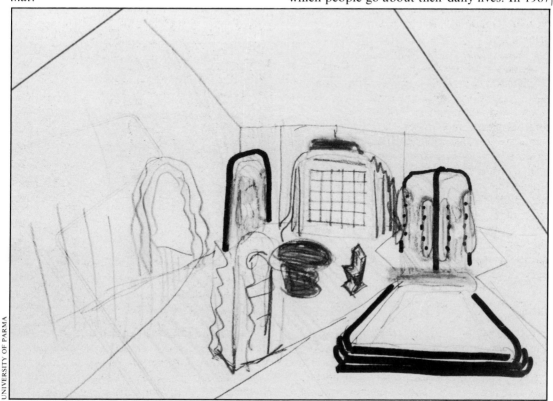

he worked on a project with Bruno Scagliola which he called 'A Room within a Room'. Its essential quality was the openness and multi-purpose nature of the space in which human interaction was the most important thing and the surroundings provided a gentle, functional background to living. Paintings and lighting formed a vital element in the atmospheric quality of the space which, nonetheless, demanded no particular set of behavioural responses.

The flexibility and neutrality of living spaces were further developed in the prototype micro-environment that Sottsass designed for the exhibition 'The New Domestic Landscape' in 1972. It consisted of a number of basic elements – grey plastic units on wheels – each of which could house a different function, for example kitchen, seat, juke-box, WC. His aim was to abolish traditional hierarchical concepts of roles within the domestic context so that new possibilities could emerge.

Alongside his interest in furniture and living environments, Sottsass intensified his interest in ceramics at this time, finding here a medium in which he could develop his more mystical ideas about the meaning and function of objects in the material world.

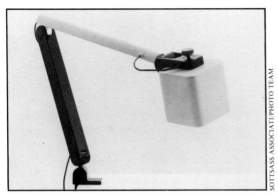

Top: Sottsass' 'Mickey Mouse' table and stools of 1971 injects humour into design.
Above: This light, designed for Erco in 1973, shows Sottsass' new 'chunky' design aesthetic.

Above: Sottsass' design for a living unit for 'Italy: The New Domestic Landscape' attempted, through its flexibility, to reject the notion of tradition in the domestic context.

*Below: These giant ceramic structures of 1967
were an attempt to evolve a contemporary
iconography of signs.*
*Bottom: At his Stockholm exhibition of 1969,
Sottsass developed his ideas about environmental
ceramics.*

SOTTSASS ASSOCIATI

SOTTSASS ASSOCIATI

The first sign that Sottsass had ceased to
think of ceramic objects as individual units
came in 1967 when he designed a series of huge
ceramic structures, 'Menhirs, Gas Pumps and
Columns, Hydrants', for an exhibition at the
Galleria Sperone in Milan. The towering phallic
constructions combined the symbolism and
myths associated with ancient civilisations with
a contemporary iconography of tall monolithic
objects such as rockets and gas pumps in the
landscape. The effect of linking the two ages
served to emphasise the timelessness of form
and its universal significance. Visually, the
pieces depended upon both a technological scale
and an aesthetic of a technological age, at the
same time making use of repetition of units and
surface patterns that had appeared in the
furniture of the previous year.

Similar large ceramic pieces were made for an
exhibition of Sottsass' work that took place in
Stockholm in 1969. He described his reasons for
using this material:

*I have made mountains of terracotta,
impossible to make, impossible to move, to
mount, to use and to pay for. Now I have made
them, I ask myself why I have made them,
because it would have been simpler to make
mountains of inflated rubber, mountains of
polyester, mountains of polystyrene and so on. It
must be because the first libraries were made with
pieces of terracotta, and the tower of Babel was
also made of terracotta. Even the Colossus in the
dream of Nebuchadnezzar had terracotta feet:
the first failures of mankind had to do with
terracotta.*[29]

It was with the series of ceramics produced in
1969 called 'Tantra' that Sottsass finally
consummated his flirtation with oriental –
particularly Indian – religions, and produced a
set of works that allied themselves totally with
the spirit of that mystical world view. Sottsass
tentatively took the term 'Tantra' from Ajit

Mookerjee's book *Tantra Art*, because 'I thought they might have something in common with that book'.[30] The series represented the continued search for a cultural context for pure form which has its roots outside European Rationalism. In appearance the pieces are extremely simple – some employ the familiar ziggurat in various different ways, and others cones and cylinders both the right way up and inverted. Their immediate function is to hold flowers, but their real meaning lies in the environmental effect of their accumulated physical presences on the space and the human beings around them.

Immediately following this experiment, Sottsass went on to design 40 more ceramic pieces, which he described as 'much more useful' and named this time 'Yantra'. Once again Ajit Mookerjee's book was called upon:

Yantra is essentially a geometrical composition; but to understand its true nature, one has to go beyond the notions of geometry and into those of dynamics. A Yantra then represents a particular force whose power or energy increases in proportion to the abstraction and precision of the diagram.[31]

The word is a key to Sottsass' idea about objects, which had now moved beyond an interest in their symbolic power to a commitment to the idea of objects as autonomous presences, existing in their own right without external reference, and influencing and changing everything that comes into contact with them.

The 'Yantra' ceramics are also flower vases, but again their meaning extends beyond the confines of their primary function. Their shapes are more varied than those of the 'Tantra' series, but depend upon the same basic language of form – the ziggurat and the cone – joined this time by the circle marked with concentric shapes on its surface. A commentator remarked that

SOTTSASS ASSOCIATI

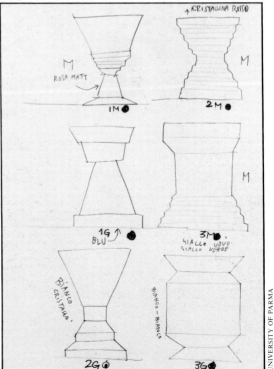

UNIVERSITY OF PARMA

they were 'inspired by Aztec sculpture and jazz-age radio receivers',[32] confirming Sottsass' interest in popular styling as a metaphor for anti-Functionalist design. The colours of the glazes are restricted to matt white, matt ochre, matt mauve, and semi-matt and very shiny black. All these colours have meanings for Sottsass that are not primarily aesthetic but symbolic – ochre is a 'silent' colour, mauve is a 'super-vulgar colour, very much liked by old prostitutes'.[33] Sottsass was aiming for a 'quality of being without quality',[34] by which he meant that he wanted to create a set of objects that had a direct sensuous and spiritual relationship with the spectator without reference to hierarchical distinctions of beauty or social status. By

SOTTSASS ASSOCIATI

Opposite: In 1969 Sottsass designed his 'Tantra' ceramics, a series suffused with an air of Indian mysticism.
Above: The 'Yantra' series of 1970 is inspired by Art Deco.

communicating with the spectator through familiar forms Sottsass hoped to side-step problems of style and discover a social meaning for the object. He had described design as a 'memorandum for the mental psychic operations necessary for liberation'.[35] As objects of contemplation in a near empty room the 'Yantra' ceramics were intended to provide a rung in the ladder that leads towards this utopian end.

A final major range of ceramics was designed in 1972. Dependent yet again upon Art Deco shapes, these giant pieces also displayed the heavy Pop, cartoon quality characteristic of Sottsass' work in the early 1970s. The links with oriental mysticism have been severed and the objects have a greater material substance, but their intended function is once again that of 'deconditioning', of removing status symbolism and the 'psycho-erotic powers of possession', this time through the mammoth scale of these sensuous teapots, streamlined coffee-pots and cups, and exotically shaped fruit bowls whose contents lie like offerings on an altar. The shapes and colours recall vacuum-formed plastics but the material used is supremely traditional.

Many of the forms and ideas that Sottsass had evolved by the mid-1970s were transferred into the glass objects that he made for Vistosi. Another minor but important range of objects that he produced in this period was a range of jewellery, which related to the human body in the same way as his furniture and ceramics related to the space around them. A necklace of 1967 worn by a girl with wild face and body make-up recalls the ritualistic and sacred ornaments worn by primitive tribes. In this area of design where decorative function outweighs practical considerations Sottsass moved even closer to an involvement with the mythological significance of archetypal forms.

In complete contrast to the ornamental function of a necklace made for the 'inner self', electronic typewriters, computers and calculators must satisfy the demands of advanced mechanisation and technical exigencies. Sottsass continued in the years following 1966 to combine these two extremes, working on the one hand on very small-scale projects made largely for his own pleasure, and on the other as a consultant to the electronics department of Olivetti.

In his designs for Olivetti Sottsass attempted a fusion of technology, aesthetics and social philosophy. He was, and is, committed to technology and its potential for liberating society, and he is not naïve where it is concerned. He realises that to design the body of a calculator one needs to know and to understand how it functions internally, and yet he still manages to keep technology at arm's length in order to see how uninitiated users will 'read' the forms of the complex mechanical objects that surround them. It is the ability to combine both knowledge and innocence that makes Sottsass such a successful industrial designer.

Sottsass allies himself firmly with the idea, put forward by Adriano Olivetti, that industry is a product of society and that it should make 'happy' products for this society upon whose energies it thrives. This means that the designer's role is to provide an image, not so much for the products but for society as a whole. All Sottsass' designs for Olivetti after

TEA POT

Left: In 1972 Sottsass designed a set of ceramic objects that asserted their presence through the monumentality of their forms. Above: From the early 1960s Sottsass had been involved with jewellery design. By the end of that decade he had developed some pieces that evoked the notion of ritual associated with primitive tribes and body decoration.

1966 operate within the framework of the object, user and society, rather than within that of industry and marketing which so many companies see as the context for design. He places the product imaginatively in the environment where it will be used, and derives from this vision many of the features by which he then defines the object that he is designing. His designs are not simply neutral forms, however. By rejecting the conventional values of items of furniture Sottsass is also protesting about their social function. For example, his witty reworking of the secretary's chair is more than just a comment on furniture traditions; it is also a protest about the routine, monotonous existence of the secretary who sits on it.

The strongest change of direction in Sottsass' work for Olivetti in this period was the move from individual objects to general systems. He explains where the impetus for this came from:

It was immediately obvious in the first years in which I worked on the ELEA that in the design of certain gigantic instruments, as electronic machines were then, or in the design of groups of machines which have a logical and operational relationship between each other, one ends up immediately designing the working environment; that is, one ends up conditioning the man who is working, not only his direct physical relationship with the instrument, but also his very much larger and more penetrating relationship with the whole act of work and the complex mechanisms of physical culture and psychic actions and reactions with the environment in which he works, the routes he takes, the emotions, the efforts, the conditionings, the liberty, the destruction, exhaustion and death.[36]

This realisation had a profound effect upon Sottsass' work for Olivetti. Among the single items that he produced were some typewriters – the Studio 45 in 1968, the Editor 5 in 1968, the Lettera 36 in 1969 and the Valentine also in

1969. The Valentine constituted the most radical departure from the conventional typewriter; with its bright red ABS plastics body and case it exerted itself as a light accessory – as necessary an appendage to contemporary living as a ball-point pen – rather than an office-bound piece of heavy machinery. In practical terms the design was innovatory in its use of a bucket case out of which the machine could be pulled down from a shelf without moving anything, and aesthetically it suggested – both by its vivid colour and its chunky, round-cornered shape – a light-hearted, witty object that would be at home in a number of environments. Sottsass emphasised the universality of the product in his advertising campaign, in which the machine was photographed in a number of elegant settings, and in his decision to retail it in boutiques and record shops as well as in the usual office equipment outlets.

The same years witnessed a vast number of computer systems components, electronic calculating machines and accounting machines coming out of the Sottsass design office, while many standard models were restyled and updated through the period. A major project was the GE 115 computer system designed in 1966 with which Sottsass redefined the visual nature of a basic computer system with its central processor and peripheral machines by integrating the wiring into the main body housing, thus eliminating the need for a false floor and creating the idea of a computer as an integrated structure rather than a series of isolated 'wardrobes'.

Attention to detail, both ergonomic and visual, characterises all the machines produced at this time. The harmonious positioning of the knobs and keys, the rounded corners of the metal body components, the clarity of the figures and general balanced construction in scale and proportions of products such as the

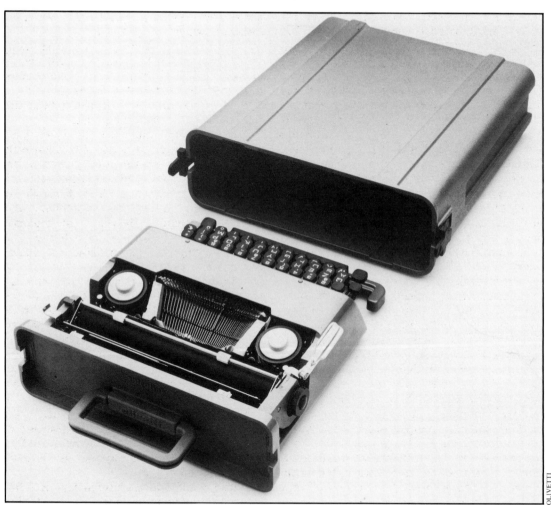

OLIVETTI

At the same time as he was developing his theories about the symbolic role of objects, Sottsass also continued to work for Olivetti. In 1969 he designed the Valentine typewriter: with its bright red plastic body this portable typewriter was intended as a appendage of contemporary life rather than a piece of office-bound machinery.

MC 23 of 1966, the TE 300 of 1968 and the A 7 of 1972 are unparalleled elsewhere.

Sottsass gradually moved towards a standard modular system, convinced that it would not restrict liberty but would in fact encourage it by allowing the machines to be manipulated by the user and not the other way round. An example of this subservience of machine to man is illustrated by the multi-viewing film exhibition system, nicknamed 'The Visual Juke-Box' that Sottsass designed in 1968 for an Olivetti stand for use at trade fairs. An important feature of the object was the space around it with benches which the viewers 'can sit on, and put down their babies and brief-cases, take off their shoes, dig into paper bags, pull out their hot dogs and popcorn and maybe even begin to talk to each other'.[37]

A commitment both to the user's total environment and to the relationship between machines in this environment based on a unified modular system led Sottsass to spend five years (1968–73) evolving a total office system called Synthesis 45, which comprised supports for the electronic equipment, desks, tables, stacking chairs, filing cabinets, acoustic screens and a number of accessories from clip-on telephone trays to umbrella stands. The system allows total flexibility and can be used in any kind of office. It is essentially passive and non-conditioning with a strong use of metal and a careful low-key colour scheme that includes pale grey for all the working surfaces, combined with crimson, terracotta, duck-egg blue and dark blue. Sottsass described the project:

The idea was to arrive as far as possible at a mean, elementary, neutral type of design, because we felt that only like this would we be able to control the general construction of the environment. We thought we should exercise a sort of 'yoga' on design, liberating shape as much as allowed us by our condition in time and space

and stripping from it every attribute, every sex-appeal deception.[38]

As with all Sottsass' designs its impact lies in its details – for example the witty, bright yellow, chunky secretary's chair with its giant hinges and screw that shares its solid base with the umbrella stand, and the use of pale blue on the filing cabinets to reduce their bulk.

This incursion into the total working environment reinforced Sottsass' concern with man's relationship with the objects with which he works and lives, and with the need for industry to provide a neutral backcloth to society rather than imposing on humanity the ethic of production. This ethic, he thought, eliminates the non-rational activities of reflection and meditation, both of them prerequisites of personal liberty.

The realism of Sottsass' work for Olivetti was paralleled by a retreat from the finished object towards fantastic visions of the future which proposed completely new structures for society and for the place of industry, architecture and design within it. Sottsass had become increasingly disillusioned with the impact that design can make upon society and saw the need for a new attitude towards the environment as a whole. The Counter Design movement had grown out of Sottsass' unease. He described it simply as 'a means of taking conscience, to feel and understand that the way the system functions today is not ideal.'[39]

Sketching and drawing have always been for Sottsass a primary means of expression. All his designs start life as quick outlines on a sketch pad, rapidly and intuitively realised in a free-hand style with a pencil, pen or coloured crayon. This instinctive approach towards the creation of form came into its own in the utopian visions of the 1970s. In the series of hand-coloured lithographs entitled 'The Planet as Festival' of 1972, urban life as we know it is

Below: The T.E. 315 teleprinter shows Sottsass' attention to visual detail and concern for ergonomics.
Right: In 1968 Sottsass designed a multi-viewing film exhibition system for Olivetti which he called 'The Visual Juke-Box'.
Below right: Sottsass' bright yellow secretary's chair was designed in 1973. With its chunky shapes and giant hinges it contains an element of humour usually missing from the office environment.

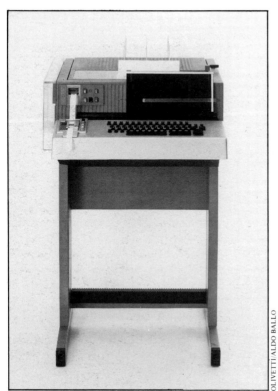

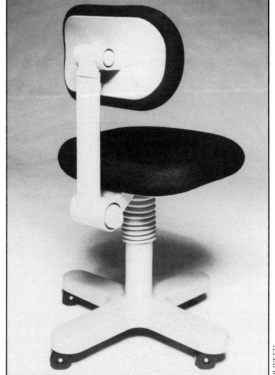

SOTTSASS ASSOCIATI

Left: One of the most important aspects of Sottsass' work in the early 1970s were his utopian depictions of future societies. His lithographic series entitled 'The Planet as Festival' of 1972 envisaged a new environment in which man and nature are reunited.
Below: Synthesis 45 was Sottsass' first large-scale office system, designed for Olivetti in the late 1960s and early 1970s. Its essence was flexibility and he evolved a low-key colour scheme to encourage the users to assert themselves within the environment.

OLIVETTI/ALDO BALLO

rejected in favour of a new environment where man and nature are reunited; pop comic-book style is combined with Dadaistic and Surrealistic graphic techniques and imagery. (Beyond the realms of fine art, the real context for this work is that of visionary architecture as developed in England by the Archigram group, in Germany by Frei Otto, and in America by Buckminster Fuller and Paolo Soleri.) 'The Planet as Festival' is inhabited by an invisible population, all of whom can exist as 'artisan-artists' using 'super-instruments': the logical culmination of Sottsass' commitment to the life of the senses in preference to the life of reason.

Sottsass wrote about the need to think in terms of utopias:

I thought there was no architecture left for me to draw; I mean that there is no architecture left to propose, either as Andrea Branzi aptly says, 'as a model for society' or to put in the hands of society as 'a psychomotor activity'. All that was left to me was to imagine architecture designed by others, 'the others'. Maybe one day they will happen to modify the use of architecture. Maybe they will design caravanserai for the wild, seasonal gatherings of tribes from every part of the planet, or festival halls. Maybe they will design rafts for trips up rivers or stadiums for land or sky observation.[40]

Sexual imagery and humour pervade all Sottsass' utopian works as supreme surreal metaphors of Anti-Rationalism. His 'Porno-graphic Architecture' series of 1973 includes an image of a maternity school housed in two giant breasts, and an 'airport for a millipede' is depicted in a series of photographs of 1976 entitled 'Necessity of Animals'. Other series, including a set of photomontages of 1976 entitled 'Project for the Destruction of Objects', 'The Destiny of Man' of the same year and 'Nonsense Architecture' of 1977, are further metaphorical statements about the mean-

inglessness of design and architecture in a world dominated by production and consumerism.

In the closing years of the 1970s, Sottsass worked on alternative environments that were responses to the world's decreasing natural resources. His project for the conservation and recycling of the Kunstgewerbemuseum in West Berlin bears witness to this concern.

During the 1970s the world was able to catch up with Sottsass; exhibitions, magazine articles and conferences treated him as the 'guru' of radical design, thinking, perhaps, that his creative career had reached a plateau and that his 'wild' days were over. In reality Sottsass was gathering strength for a new burst of energy which exploded at the end of the decade with a new wave of avant-garde experimentation that took the Italian design mainstream by storm.

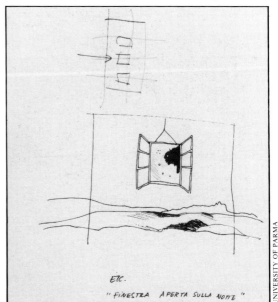

'Construction in the Open' of 1974 is an example of Sottsass' conceptual projects of the mid-1970s.

Post-Radicalism

By the end of the 1970s Italian design had consolidated its position on the world market. The giants from the late 1960s continued to supply the major industries with high quality designs – among them Magistretti for Cassina, Zanuso for Brionvega and Achille Castiglioni for Flos; the numerous design magazines (which had proliferated at an astonishing rate since the mid-1960s) continued to provide a sophisticated, high-gloss back-up for the Italian 'star system' of designers; and Italian designers continued to have a special reputation for quality and style in the world market. In spite of the insecurities of Italian political, economic and cultural life, design sustained its position at the heart of Italian manufacturing.

CASSINA

Magistretti's 'Sindbad' chair, produced by Cassina in 1981, shows a continued interest in innovation while still reflecting the good taste of the Milanese design establishment.

Automobile design was a particular area of expertise. Giorgio Giugiaro, with his company Italdesign, was employed by the German Volkswagen company to develop a new aesthetic for the private car. His solution – the VW Golf – has influenced many other designs since its appearance in the early 1970s. More recently his car for Fiat – the Panda – shows how Italy's eminence in the field of automobile design has continued into the 1980s. The radicalism of this small car, which was designed from the inside out and determined by economy of space and efficiency of fuel consumption, has provided a new concise image for the modern car.

Many Italian designers who began work in the post-war years have, in recent years, reached

DESIGN COUNCIL RICHARD DAVIES

VOLKSWAGEN

Opposite, top: Giugiaro's Fiat Panda shows typical Italian flair for finding images for the contemporary world.
Opposite, bottom: Giugiaro designed the Volkswagen Golf in the early 1970s.
Below: Gaetano Pesce's 'Manhattan Sunrise' seating was produced by Cassina in 1980.
Bottom: Mario Bellini's furniture design for B & B Italia was produced in 1981.

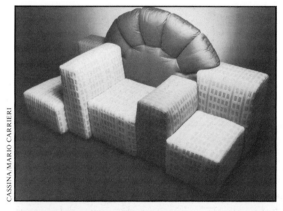

CASSINA/MARIO CARRIERI

a new level of maturity. Learning much from the radical movements of the early 1970s, Mario Bellini is one such designer. He has moved from the strictly mechanistic attitude expressed by the work he did for Olivetti in the 1960s to a much fuller philosophy of design that embraces all the proposals of the Post-Modern Movement. Gaetano Pesce continues his individualistic, surrealistic pokes at the design establishment; his Manhattan Sunset furniture was produced by Cassina in 1979.

In spite of these areas of strength, mainstream design in Italy had not really changed radically since the late 1960s. It had simply been expertly packaged and sold to the rest of the world. The courage of former years had been replaced by caution – the premature closure of the 1974 Triennale had shaken the confidence of many – and the fear of loss of prestige. A preponderance of marble tables and leather sofas at recent furniture shows and of black box electronic equipment in the mainstream design area bear witness to this reactionary attitude.

B & B ITALIA

What is most comforting about Ettore Sottsass' most recent work is that he still continues to shock. Now in his mid-sixties, the image of the rebellious, avant-garde, anti-establishment figure is gloriously maintained. Sottsass has proven in the last couple of years that middle age is no enemy of imagination and innovation and he has continued to develop his creative consciousness, producing designs that demonstrate this constant evolution.

Studio Alchymia was formed in 1976 by Alessandro Guerriero as a centre for innovatory design that would be manufactured and sold rather than just imagined. It rapidly attracted into its ranks members of the radical groups of the late 1960s, including Alessandro Mendini – by the late 1970s editor of both *Domus* and the more avant-garde *Modo* – who used Studio Alchymia as a base from which to make forays into radical furniture. He was soon joined by Andrea Branzi – late of Superstudio, Ettore Sottsass and some members of a new generation of radical designers, among them Michele de Lucchi, Paola Navone and Daniele Puppa.

By the late 1970s Sottsass had reached a new plateau in his creative development: his design office for Olivetti – now occupied exclusively with office furniture and systems – had moved

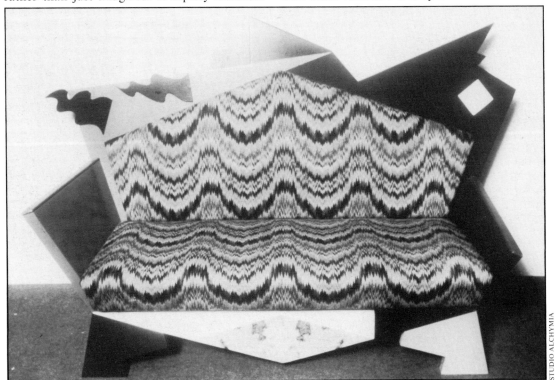

STUDIO ALCHYMIA

In his 'Kandissi' chair for Studio Alchymia, Alessandro Mendini has turned fine art into kitsch. This piece formed part of the 'BauHaus 1' collection of 1980.

from the Via Manzoni to the Corso Venezia; his own architectural and design company – Sottsass Associati – was ensconced in the Via Borgonuovo and occupied with a series of international projects; he had exhibited his work in Germany, France, Jerusalem and Australia, and had spoken at numerous international design conferences. Just when there were signs that he might be settling into a routine, the challenge presented by the Alchymia experiment fired Sottsass into a new and even more energetic phase of creative activity.

Mendini was and is the spokesman for Studio Alchymia and his texts speak of a movement in furniture design which is 'post-radical' or 'post-avant-garde'. This was round two of the radical movement in Italian design and it raised a number of fundamental questions which up until then had only been hinted at. In the BauHaus 1 series of 1979 and the BauHaus 2 series of 1980 Mendini and his colleagues explored the aesthetic possibilities of the mass environment, exploiting the decorative potential of its imagery. The abstract patterns on the plastic-laminated surfaces of the bizarre sofas, bookcases, tables in these series owe their origins to banal objects from the 1950s or

STUDIO ALCHYMIA

Andrea Branzi has reworked, ironically, some classic Italian designs from the 1930s in his series of furniture for Studio Alchymia. This buffet was designed in 1980.

STUDIO ALCHYMIA

*Left: Paola Navone's chest of drawers for
Studio Alchymia makes use of a plastic
laminate pattern from the 1950s.*
*Below left: Sottsass' glass for Vistosi from the
early 1970s contains many of his preoccupations
of those years. This model of 1972 is called
'Orsete'.*
*Below: Sottsass' chair for Studio Alchymia
is made entirely of industrial materials – plastic
laminate and metal.*
*Opposite, top left: This witty lamp for Stilnovo
brings Sottsass' familiar 'Mickey Mouse'
imagery into product design.*
*Opposite, top right: One of Sottsass' personal
projects of the late 1970s was the design of a
customised car for Fiorucci.*
*Opposite, bottom: Among Mario Bellini's most
sophisticated designs was his wedge-shaped
'Yamaha' cassette deck of 1975.*

VETRERIA VISTOSI/ALDO BALLO

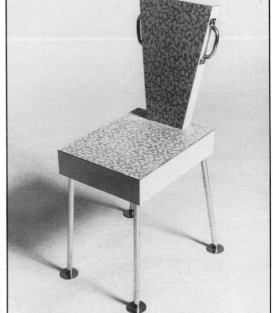

STUDIO ALCHYMIA

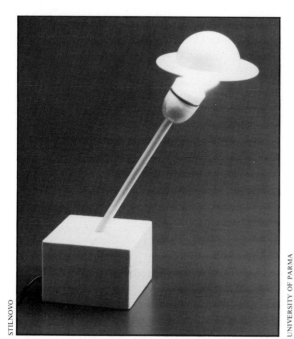

STILNOVO

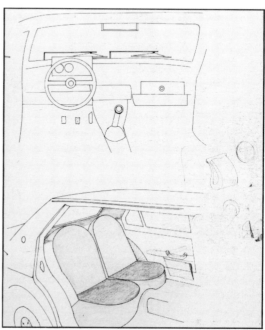

UNIVERSITY OF PARMA

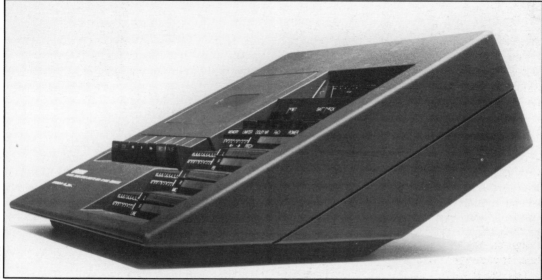

OLIVETTI

to fine-art sources. While Mendini made intellectual art-historical references and called upon 'kitsch' as the rationale behind his designs, and Branzi made ironical statements about the Modern Movement in his strange shelving systems and seats, Sottsass went one step further, moving beyond self-consciousness and making optimistic pieces of furniture that simply echoed the 'non-cultural' environment of the 1950s:

So I have chosen textures like the grit and the mosaics of public conveniences in the underground stations of big cities, like the tight wire netting of suburban fences, or like the spongy paper of government account books ... I should have been able to propose some sort of iconography of non-culture.[41]

This enthusiastic appropriation of textures and patterns from the everyday environment was accompanied by an exploitation of banal, man-made materials – airport rubber floors, plastic laminate ('a material with no uncertainties'[42]), and 'the galvanised sheet used on electrical appliances which is usually hidden'.[43]

Far from decrying the tastelessness of the mass environment, Sottsass was celebrating the ordinariness and honesty of the banal. On one level he was stepping on the nostalgia bandwagon, on another he was opening himself to the force of popular taste and integrating it into his personal vision of design. In selecting patterns originated in the 1950s – the heroic period of Italian design when design, society and culture had a truly sympathetic relationship with each other – Sottsass had come full circle, making references to designs that he could have created himself in the early years of his career. A personal touch is included in one of the laminates from 1980 which revives an abstract design by Mario Radice, the father of Sottsass' close friend, Barbara Radice.

The visual sensationalism and surreal quality

of his designs – such as the leaning bookcase, the trembling table and the chair with handles – inspired a good deal of press and public reaction. Studio Alchymia has succeeded in reviving the possibility of an 'alternative' design movement in Italy.

The gulf between Mendini's essential pessimism about the power of objects to change society, and Sottsass' deep commitment to the importance of creativity as a social force, led to a philosophical schism between Studio Alchymia designers. This, in turn, caused Sottsass to break away and form his own experimental design company. In the late summer of 1981 'Memphis' was launched in Milan amid gasps of astonishment. It was named Memphis for several reasons:

A name mentioned in numerous songs ... MEMPHIS, Tennessee, birthplace of W.C. Hardy, father of the blues, of Elvis Presley, father of rock 'n' roll. MEMPHIS, ancient capital of Egypt and site of the great temple of the god Ptah, artist among the gods, 'he who creates works of art'.[44]

The venture combined Sottsass' fascination with ancient civilisations with his commitment to contemporary 'pop' culture. Presented by a group of international designers – contributions came from Japan, the USA, England and Spain as well as from Italy – the objects designed for Memphis are characterised by vivid colour and decoration, combined with a concern for function and a use of industrial materials. Even Peter Shire's bizarre ceramic sculptures are teapots that can pour tea. Although Memphis opened like an avant-garde art gallery the objects it offers for sale are tables, chairs, wardrobes, shelves, and so on. Like the designs for Alchymia, Memphis prototypes are hand made (the furniture-maker Renzo Brugola has been with Sottsass for many years), but the materials employed – plastic laminates, aluminium and glass among them – are industrial materials, well suited to production in mass should the market make such demands.

Memphis furniture is non-intellectual, 'positive propositive rather than critical',[45] and intended to be included in any interior, regardless of style. As such, it diverges from the more self-conscious intellectualism of the other Milanese radical groups. It remains, instead, within the intuitive, optimistic tradition that Sottsass has established through the past two decades. He writes about Memphis with the confidence that stems from maturity:

By dint of walking among the areas of the uncertain (due to a certain mistrust), by dint of conversing with metaphor and utopia (to understand something more) and by keeping out of the way (certainly due to an innate calmness), we now find we have gained some experience; we have become good explorers. Maybe we can navigate wide, dangerous rivers, and advance into jungles where no-one has ever set foot. There is absolutely no need for concern . . . our fear of the past is gone, and so is our still more aggressive fear of the future.[46]

By 1981 Sottsass had survived the traumas of creative struggle and reached a level of maturity and self-fulfilment that is communicated to the world by Memphis. As an experiment it is very daring and as a new attitude towards design which no longer comments on the past but begins again, 'ex novo', it is unequalled. It underlines Sottsass' truly radical stance – which involves rethinking the meaning as well as the forms of design – and his ability to move beyond the questions and criticisms raised by rejecting the status quo and towards a new, positive statement that proposes a new life for the designed object. Memphis confirms that, for Sottsass:

Design is not finished with a more or less well placed chrome trim or in some novelty more or

less new, but one starts to understand that design is above all a conscious act, an act of clarification, of distension, of decanting the complex tangle of trajectories, of actions and reactions of every sort which surround the presence of the instrument.[47]

MEMPHIS/PETER OGILVIE

Among the designers who worked with Sottsass on the Memphis project was Michele de Lucchi. His Op Art-inspired, anthropomorphic coffee table, called 'Kristall', expresses de Lucchi's interest in turning products into toys.

Below: Paola Navone's coat hanger for Memphis is called 'Versilia'.
Below right and opposite, top: Sottsass' designs for Memphis recall many of his preoccupations from the past three decades. His interest in decoration, radical shapes and industrial materials has recurred throughout his career, and Memphis brings together many of his ideas *and feelings about the role of design in everyday life. The 'Treetops' lamp, 'Mandarin' table and 'Carlton' bookcase were designed in 1981.*
Opposite, bottom: Along with Michele de Lucchi, George Sowden has worked in Sottsass' Olivetti office for a number of years. His 'Chelsea' bed for Memphis is covered by a fabric designed by Nathalie du Pasquier.

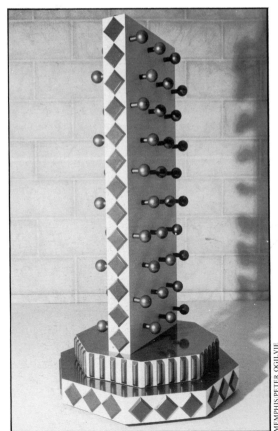

MEMPHIS/PETER OGILVIE

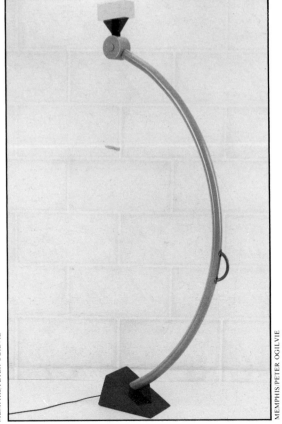

MEMPHIS/PETER OGILVIE

MEMPHIS/PETER OGILVIE

MEMPHIS/PETER OGILVIE

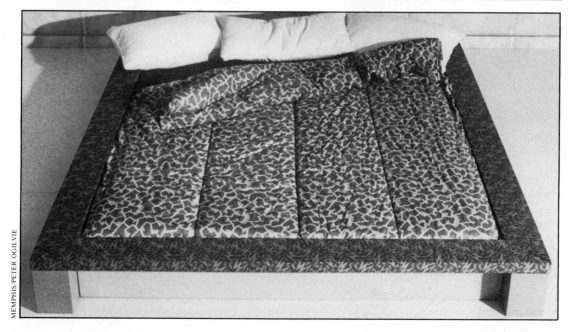

MEMPHIS/PETER OGILVIE

Conclusion

Ettore Sottsass Jnr still lives and works in the heart of Milan. He continues to travel extensively, having returned to the USA and India several times and visited, among other places, Polynesia, North Africa, South America and, most recently, Japan where he was fascinated by the primitive cultures that he discovered. The inspiration that he experiences by entering an alien culture and feeling the power of new visual environments plays a vital part in his continued creativity. After a recent trip to Polynesia he remarked on his return to Milan that it was difficult to readjust from looking at the horizon several hundred feet away to the ten square feet that form our personal space in Europe.

Sottsass continues to devour life and to transpose his experiences into visual form. In addition to the furniture for Studio Alchymia and the more recent Memphis pieces, he still proposes projects for 'alternative architecture'; collaborates, through his design company, with firms in Italy and abroad – recent projects include glass for Fontana Arte, stainless steel for Alessi, designs for Croff, a camper for Fiat and furniture for Zanotta; works on personal experiments such as the bizarre customised Alfa Romeo designed for Fiorucci and more recently jewellery for a Japanese company; and continues to expound his ever-developing philosophy of design that moves nearer and nearer towards a philosophy of life. To many he is still an enigmatic figure, as his perceptions remain highly personalised and always intuitive, never rational (he calls himself a stupid peasant rather than an intellectual).

There is a consistency in Sottsass' work that extends beyond the re-utilisation in many of his designs for Memphis of numerous elements of the design vocabulary he has developed over the past 25 years. It lies instead in his continued commitment to the combined powers of reason and intuition and in his sustained vision of objects as standing for more than their mere material selves. Throughout his career Sottsass has defined objects as metaphors. Alone they are meaningless, and are only imbued with significance by the context of human life and use. The extent to which Sottsass articulates and manipulates this potential meaning is the measure of his strength and his genius. Through his development of a highly sophisticated, articulate design language he has suggested ways of radically redefining the twentieth-century consumer object.

As with any avant-garde cultural movement, Sottsass is often misunderstood and frequently attacked. The most common accusation is that he thinks and acts like a fine artist rather than a designer. What Sottsass has in fact achieved is to have raised the status of design to that of a conceptual rather than a manual skill and to have eroded distinctions between fine art and design. Sottsass is ultimately less interested in reaching a wide public than in finding possible ways in which design can become a pure communication medium between man and the physical world rather than a mere adjunct of industry and commerce. In attempting to rid design of such ideological impurities Sottsass has retained a level of integrity unmatched elsewhere in the design world. It is this that attracts the student of design to him and that has earned him his world-wide reputation.

Sottsass is undoubtedly still the most radical of contemporary designers; few others have succeeded in sidestepping the dictates of style, taste, industry and the market. He opens up the possibility of a new interaction between man and his environment. As he wrote in the catalogue to the Jerusalem exhibition:

The message is not in the quantity of objects, or in their design, but in communication.[48]

Within the context of Post-Modernism – that

Conclusion

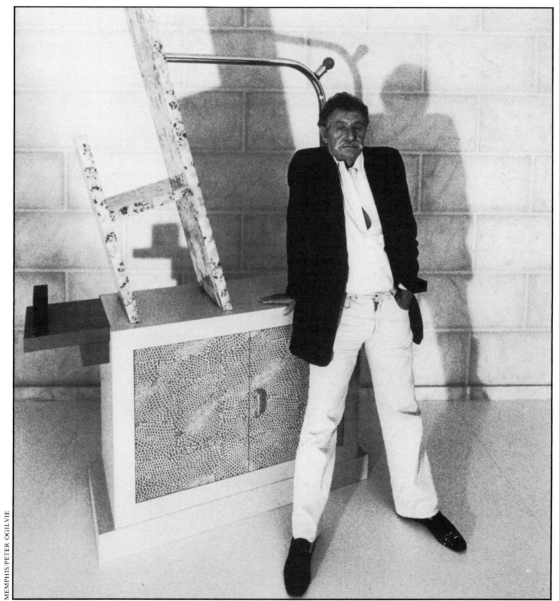

MEMPHIS/PETER OGILVIE

Ettore Sottsass Jnr standing in front of 'Beverley', one of his most bizarre designs for Memphis.

recent movement in architecture and design that seeks to reject the monolithic nature of pre-war Modernism – Sottsass is a seminal figure, as he has accepted this challenge several times over, utilising many different strategies to undermine the autocracy of Functionalism. In the words of Mendini:

The historic role that Sottsass plays in the Modern Movement is that of having been a forerunner in opening the first cultural debate on function and language, in the wrongdoings and failures of all the models of rationalism, of having become 'the person people who are involved with underground architecture all over the world feel attracted to and identify with'. No orthodoxy, no ideology, no allegory, no moral motivation. Projects as natural phenomena, as pure acts of immediate release.[49]

While Memphis continues to shock and puzzle the Milanese design establishment, Sottsass is already preparing new projects to stretch both the intellects and imaginations of his contemporaries. In his words:

I am a designer and want to design things. What else would I do? Go fishing?[50]

Some Biographical Details

1917   Born in Innsbruck of a family from the Trentino. Childhood spent in Trento where his father was responsible for the reconstruction of villages destroyed in the First World War.

1928   Moved to Turin with his parents.

1934   Enrolled at the School of Architecture in the Polytechnic of Turin.

1936   Travelled to Paris.

1937   Began publishing articles about art and interior decoration.

1939   Graduated from the Polytechnic of Turin.

1939   Joined the services as a soldier.

1943   Served with the troops in Montenegro.

1945   Joined the Giuseppe Pagano group of architects in Turin.

1946   Moved to Milan and began work as a designer.

1946   Organised, with Bruno Munari, the first show of abstract art in Milan.

1947   Contributed to the Eighth Triennale.

1948   Began work on the INA-CASA scheme for the architectural reconstruction of Novara and Savona.

1949   Married Fernanda Pivano (Nanda).

1951   Contributed to the Ninth Triennale.

1954   Contributed to the Tenth Triennale.

1956   Travelled to the USA and worked in the studio of George Nelson.

1957   Contributed to the Eleventh Triennale.

1957–8 Began his collaboration with the Olivetti Company.

1958–9 Designed ELEA 9003 computer, which marked his incursion into industrial design.

1960   Contributed to the Twelfth Triennale.

1961   Travelled to India.

1962   Suffered a severe kidney illness and went to the USA for treatment.

1965–6 Designed series of furniture for Poltronova which influenced the Counter-Design Movement of these years.

1968   Awarded an honorary degree at the Royal College of Art in London.

1969–70 Designed sets of ceramics influenced by Indian mysticism.

1969   Exhibition of his ceramics in Stockholm.

1969   Designed the Valentine typewriter, the last of his consumer products for Olivetti.

1970   Met Eulalia Grau in Barcelona with whom he lived for five years.

1972   Participated in the 'New Domestic Landscape' exhibition at the Museum of Modern Art in New York.

1973   Exhibition in Minneapolis.

1975   Founder member of 'Global Tools' group.

1975–7 Worked with a group of young architects including Andrea Branzi.

1976   Exhibited work in Berlin, Vienna and Paris.

1976   Exhibited 'Designs for the Destiny of Man' in New York.

1976   Met Barbara Radice, with whom he is now living.

1977–9 Worked on floppy discs for Olivetti.

1979   Exhibited work in Jerusalem and Australia.

1979   Guest speaker at ICSID conference in Mexico.

1979   Began work with the Studio Alchymia group.

1980   Formed Sottsass Associati in partnership with four young architects.

1980   Worked on 'BauHaus 1' collection for Studio Alchymia.

1981   Opened Memphis.

1981   Exhibited and travelled in Japan.

References

1 E. Sottsass Jnr, lecture given at Design and Industries Association Annual Conference, London, April 1979, unpublished.
2 A. Mendini, Introduction to F. di Castro (ed), *Sottsass' Scrapbook*, Casabella, Milan, 1976, p6.
3 E. Rogers, Editorial in *Domus*, January 1946, p3.
4 E. Rogers, quoting P. Bottini in 'Experience from the Eighth Triennale' in *Domus*, July 1947, p1.
5 W.D. Teague, 'An Italian Shopping Trip' in *Interiors*, November 1950, p199.
6 E. Sottsass Jnr, 'Forme, Arredamenti, Oggetti' in *Domus*, no 279, 1953, p29.
7 E. Sottsass Jnr, 'Forme asimmetriche e leggere' in *Domus*, no 296, 1954, p54.
8 M. Zanuso, 'Two Chairs' in *Australian Lectures*, Industrial Design Council of Australia, 1971, p28.
9 G. Ponti, Editorial in *Domus*, January 1948, p3.
10 J. Colombo, in exhibition catalogue *Qu'est-ce que le design*? Centre de Création Industrielle, Paris, 1969, p27.
11 Report presented at exhibition 'New Designs for Italian Furniture', Milan, March 1960, quoted in E. Ambasz (ed), *Italy: The New Domestic Landscape*, Museum of Modern Art, New York, 1972.
12 E. Sottsass Jnr, 'Interiors: Composition of Walls' in *Domus*, no 358, 1959, p13.
13 E. Sottsass Jnr, 'A New Bar in Genoa' in *Domus*, no 376, 1961, p33.
14 E. Sottsass Jnr, 'Experience with Ceramics' in *Domus*, no 489, 1970, p56.
15 E. Sottsass Jnr, 'The Ceramics of Darkness' in *Domus*, no 409, 1963, p45.
16 E. Sottsass Jnr, 'Offerta a Siva' in *Domus*, no 422, 1965, p49.
17 E. Sottsass Jnr, notes for a lecture.
18 E. Sottsass Jnr, 'How to Survive with a Company, Perhaps', (unpublished lecture).
19 E. Sottsass Jnr, 'Una Macchina Scatola' in *Domus*, no 427, 1965, p43.
20 A. De Angelis, 'Anti-Design' quoted in F. Raggi, 'Radical Story' in *Casabella*, no 382, 1973, p39.
21 F. Raggi, 'Radical Story' in *Casabella*, no 382, 1973, p40.
22 *Ibid*, p45.
23 *Op cit* (14), p55.
24 *Ibid*.
25 *Op cit* (2), p6.
26 E. Sottsass Jnr, catalogue to exhibition 'Ettore Sottsass Jnr' at the Israel Museum, Jerusalem, Spring 1978.
27 E. Sottsass Jnr, 'Katalogo Mobili 1966' in *Domus*, no 449, 1967, p39.
28 E. Sottsass Jnr, 'Could Anything be More Ridiculous?' in *Design*, no 262, 1970, p29.
29 E. Sottsass Jnr, 'Sottsass a Stoccalma' in *Domus*, May 1969, p47.
30 E. Sottsass Jnr, 'Ceramiche Tantriche' in *Domus*, no 478, 1969, p33.
31 *Op cit* (14), p56.
32 *Ibid*.
33 *Op cit* (28), p30.
34 *Ibid*, p35.
35 *Op cit* (14), p56.
36 *Op cit* (18).
37 B.A., 'Olivetti's Visual Juke-Box' in *Industrial Design*, March 1969, p32.
38 A. Best, 'Of Machines and Men' in *Design*, January 1973, p52.
39 E. Sottsass Jnr, from lecture notes.
40 E. Sottsass Jnr, 'The Planet as Festival' in *Design Quarterly*, no 89, Minnesota, 1973.
41 E. Sottsass Jnr, Introduction to *Catalogue for Decorative Furniture in Modern Style 1979–80*, Studio Forma/Alchymia, 1980.
42 *Ibid*.
43 *Ibid*.
44 B. Radice, press release for Memphis, Summer 1981.
45 B. Radice (ed), *Memphis: The New International Style*, Electa, Milan, 1981, p5.
46 *Ibid*, p7.
47 *Op cit* (18).
48 *Op cit* (26).
49 *Op cit* (2), p7.
50 *Op cit* (26).

Select Bibliography

There are very few books in English that concern themselves with post-war Italian design. Extensive information is available only in the catalogue, edited by Emilio Ambasz, that accompanied the exhibition of Italian design at the Museum of Modern Art, New York, *Italy: The New Domestic Landscape* (The Museum of Modern Art, New York, in collaboration with Centro Di, Florence, 1972).

There are isolated articles in English-language periodicals that deal with Italian design in the post-war period. These include B. Allen, 'Italy's New Idiom' in *Industrial Design* (New York, October 1967); J.R.G., 'Italian Design in the 60s: A decade and a half' in *Industrial Design* (New York, May 1972); J.F.K. Henrion, 'Italian Journey' in *Design* (London, January 1949); C. Jencks, 'The Supersensualists' in *Architectural Design* (London, June 1971 and January 1972); and W.D. Teague, ' An Italian Shopping Trip' in *Interiors* (New York, November 1950).

In Italian there is inevitably more choice. The best book on the subject is P. Fossati, *Il Design in Italia 1945–1972* (Einaudi, Turin, 1972), closely followed by A. Grassi and A. Pansera, *Atlante del Design Italiano 1940–1980* (Gruppo Editoriale Fabbri, Milan, 1980). Other useful books include G. Dorfles, *Introduzione al disegno industriale* (Einaudi, Turin, 1972), and P. Navoni and B. Orlandoni, *Archittetura 'radicale'* (Documenti di Casabella, Milan, 1974), which documents the movement known as 'Counter-Design'. A useful article is V. Gregotti, 'Per una storia del design italiano' in *Ottagono* (nos 32, 33, 34, Milan, 1974–5), and the magazines *Domus, Casabella, Stile Industria* and *Modo* (all published in Milan) all provide vital source material for a study of Italian post-war design.

The life and work of Ettore Sottsass Jnr are quite well documented, mostly in Italian and particularly in the magazines mentioned above, which also contain a large number of his own writings. There is only one book, published in Italy but containing an English translation, that is exclusively about Sottsass: Federica di Castro (ed), *Sottsass' Scrapbook* (Documenti di Casabella, Milan, 1976), and this can be consulted for a more complete list of writings by and about Sottsass. The best account of the first half of his career is in Italian: P.C. Santini, 'Introduzione ad Ettore Sottsass' in *Zodiac,* (no 11, Milan, 1963). Catalogues that have accompanied exhibitions of his work are valuable sources of information and include *Miljo for en ny Planet* (National Museum, Stockholm, 1969); 'Sottsass, Superstudio: Mindscapes', published in *Design Quarterly,* (no 89, Minneapolis, Minnesota, 1973); *Ettore Sottsass Jr, de l'objet fini à la fin de l'objet* (Centre de Création Industrielle, Paris, 1976); and *Ettore Sottsass Jr* (The Israel Museum, Jerusalem, 1978). Recently two books have been published to accompany his new avant-garde furniture: E. Sottsass, *Catalogue for Decorative Furniture in Modern Style 1979–80* (Studio Forma/Alchymia, Milan, 1980), and B. Radice (ed), *Memphis: The New International Style* (Electa, Milan, 1981).

Several articles in English-language periodicals have focused upon Sottsass and his work. These include A. Best, 'For the Archetypal Woman' in *Design* (no 249, London, 1969); A. Best, 'Medium Cool Message' in *Design* (no 262, London, 1970); A. Best, 'Of Machines and Men: Olivetti's Sistema 45' in *Design* (no 237, London, September 1968); D. Danes, 'Joy of a Top Price Light: German Lighting Manufacturer Erco' in *Design* (no 298, London, 1973); J.R.G., 'Turning On' in *Industrial Design* (New York, July 1970); P. Sparke, 'A Peasant Genius' in *Design* (London, June 1981); T. Trini 'Ceramics 67' in *Domus* (no 455, Milan, 1967); and R. Waterhouse, 'A Valentine for your Thoughts' in *Design* (no 250, London, 1969).

Throughout his career Sottsass has written extensively, mostly in *Domus,* about his own work and travels. Pieces translated into English include 'Could Anything be More Ridiculous?' in *Design* (no 262, London, 1970); 'Experience with Ceramics' in *Domus* (no 489, Milan, 1970); 'Conversations with Designers' in *Design* (London, January 1974); and 'Block Notes' in *Casabella* (no 408, Milan, 1975).

Acknowledgments

Among the numerous people who have helped me while preparing and writing this book, I would like to extend particular thanks to, of course, Ettore Sottsass himself, who talked patiently with me for many hours; also Barbara Radice, Michele de Lucchi and Marco Zanini, all of whom have known and worked with Sottsass for many years. Simona Riva at the Parma archive of drawings by Italian architects and designers was also very helpful, and I thank her for her time.

I would also like to thank friends and family who listened to all my problems and read pieces of the text, and The Design Council for its help in publishing it.